# THE MESSAGE
A Play

# THE MESSAGE
A Play

## Dilliswar Moharana

*Translated by*
## Sanjeet Kumar Das

**BLACK EAGLE BOOKS**
Dublin, USA | Bhubaneswar, India

Black Eagle Books
USA address:
7464 Wisdom Lane
Dublin, OH 43016

India address:
E/312, Trident Galaxy, Kalinga Nagar,
Bhubaneswar-751003, Odisha, India

E-mail: info@blackeaglebooks.org
Website: www.blackeaglebooks.org

First International Edition Published by
Black Eagle Books, 2024

**THE MESSAGE**
by **Dilliswar Moharana**

Translated by Sanjeet Kumar Das

Original Copyright © Dr. Dilliswar Moharana
Translation Copyright © Sanjeet Kumar Das

All rights reserved. No part of this publication may be reproduced, stored in a retrieval system, or transmitted, in any form or by any means, electronic, mechanical, photocopying, recording or otherwise without the prior permission of the publisher.

Cover & Interior Design: Ezy's Publication

ISBN- 978-1-64560-597-3 (Paperback)

Printed in the United States of America

## Author's View

The writers who follow some Western styles or celebrate foreign writers and their writings and make their writings unintelligible are considered in this country as aristocratic and intellectual. In the 1960s, some playwrights of our state suddenly wanted to show their charisma, jumping from the traditional style of writing plays. They forgot Odia culture and social issues and concentrated on the psychological analysis of a self-centered lifestyle. As those plays were a total of symbols and connected with dry wordplay, they didn't appeal to human sentiment and couldn't entertain the public. Like modern poetry, they became unintelligible and incomprehensible and lost human credibility. These plays were approved and appreciated as experimental plays in literature, but their thematic body seemed sympathetic and helpless when staged. Having seen this form, the audience was terrified and left the theatres. In this context, the commercial theatres of the state became obsolete and useless. The closing of the theatre blocked the growth of the theatrical tradition. But time's call and public thirst for the play encouraged the group theatre artists, and their performance, which suited their taste, inclined the audience towards the stage again. When this process continued in the 1980s, the introduction of T.V. in India arrested the people in the drawing room. Some people couldn't avoid the artists' requests and appeared on the stage as the audience suggested changes, such as the fast change of scenes and the plays being confined to a short duration like the T.V. serials or plays. Taking this into account and the circumference of the stage, the playwrights who wrote for Group Theatres started writing to display many scenes within a short period through minor roles. These plays were staged mainly by theatre artists, so they had some demands before the playwrights. They hoped, "Let the plays be written with strong storylines, dialogues suitable to characters, and completion of all the characters with equal importance in the play." By doing this, every artist can perform well and be rewarded in the play competitions. As I was directly associated with the 'Theatre Movement', I have scripted most of the plays in this style. You can realize this if you read the play *The Message*.

This play was first staged by artists of the famous drama institution "Dhenkanal Kalaparishad" and organized by Natyam Angul for its stage show on Natyam Natyamela in 1993. It bagged second prize to its credit. Akash Vani Cuttack broadcast this play on the radio for the first time on 25.04.1994. I would like to thank the playwright Sri Anand Chandra Pahi for helping me publish this play in book form.

This play *Bartta* (*The Message*) was awarded the Odisha Sahitya Akademi Award in 2004.

**Dilliswar Moharana**

# Proposal

**Step 'A'**

Here is the dwelling place of an extremist group. From the sounds of crickets and other insects, it is realized that it is midnight. Doctor Satya Sanatan, red-handed as the hostage, sleeps while sitting at a place. An extremist fighter named Bul occasionally visits with an AK 47 rifle. Getting an opportunity, someone throws a cloth bag in the room. The Doctor gets up. Looking around, he goes to check what that bag contains minutely. After opening the bag, he finds a torch light, two diaries, some old inland letters, and an envelope. While opening the bag, he also sees a letter written on red paper. He lights his torch to read that letter. The letter's language is heard in Arun's voice from the background.

Arun: (Voice) We have changed our plan at the last moment. You first step out of this camp with Alok. Surabhi and I will join you later. The clue to our plan is known to the Commander. He may not allow us to leave this place, but we will try our best. We will fail. He might have heard something about me from Surabhi, but that's not absolute. This bag contains personal letters communicated between Surabhi and me and some emotional diaries. You will write something about us based on the letter, diary, and what you have heard from us directly and publish it. Then, the play

*The message* will reach crores of youth, and the child you are accompanying will grow up and know about us one day.

[The creak of the Watchman's boot is heard. Doctor Satya Sanathan hides the bag with the letter and does the act of sleeping. Watchman comes and goes. Doctor Satya Sanatan looks at the Watchman's return…The stage light is off.]

## Step 'B'

[In the darkness, the ear-blasting sound of the huge explosion and cries of distress are heard. After a while, everything normalized. The sight of a burning fire is only seen on the back screen. On the front stage, Doctor Satya Sanatan and Alok are spotted walking in a particular light circle. The doctor shoulders a previously described bag. The sound of a train nearing is heard. Doctor Satyasanatan and Alok start running. The stage lights are off.]

## Step 'C'

[The train seems to reach the station in the darkness and halts, and the hawkers call if the people want tea, coffee, and cigarettes. The next moment, the train leaves the station with the sound of bells and whistles.

After the stage light, Doctor Satya Sanatan and Alok are marked as sitting in the running train, and the bag is hooked near the window panel.

Two symbolic windows are kept on one side of the compartment. On the other side of the window on the window along with the scenery of trees, buildings, and hills, the rhythmic sound of the train can be used to make the scene livelier and more realistic.

The train runs faster. Satya Sanatan looks at the bag. Again, he recollects some portions of the letter.]

Arun: In that bag are some personal letters communicated between Surabhi and me and some writings emotionally penned in my diaries. Letter, diary, and what you have heard from us are the only stuff for you to write about us and will publish too.

[Doctor Satya Sanatan removes the bag from the hook and reads the bundle of letters and the diary. The train lights gradually diminish as soon as the train runs fast.]

**Dilliswar Moharana**

# Translator's View

Dilliswar Moharana is one of the leading playwrights of Contemporary Odia literature. I have translated his Odisha Sahitya Akademi Award 2004-winning play *Bartta* into English as *The Message*. The play is aptly didactic in its approach to bring about social reformation.

The play's plot unfolds with the protagonist, Arun, a First Class First Post Graduate student. Despite his good academic record, he could not get a job at the university. Average students get jobs in society due to political interference. Frustrated with the social system, he joins the Save India Fighter Organization (S.I.F.O.), an extremist group. The senior Freedom Fighter, Sugreeva Nayak's daughter, Surabhi, is Arun's crush. Their love gets approved by their parents. When her innocence is ruined by the associates of the political leaders Anadi Babu and Paramapriya Babu, she joins the S.I.F.O. group. Her illegitimate child, Alok, is brought to the S.I.F.O. Camp. The theme revolves around the character of Arun, who becomes a S.I.F.O. Fighter and is later convinced to join the mainstream of society. The commander's dialogue matters here, "There are multiple entrance points, but no exit point to the extremists' camp. Nobody can return from this organization with life." Arun and his love Surabhi lose their lives while attempting to leave the camp towards the end of the play.

When Doctor Satya Sanatan is kidnapped to their camp, his strong personality influences the fighters. He interacts with the S.I.F.O. Fighter Arun.

Arun asks Doctor Satya Sanatan, "What do you mean by 'Revolution'?" Satya Sanatan, a well-known writer, and a doctor, responds to Arun as follows: It is the transformation of an individual from the path of degeneration to righteousness, the correction of wrong to right, and the cultural change from horror to loveliness and the eternal. Revolution is not the slogan for an overnight storm. It can't be achieved in a day. It needs mental preparedness and strong perseverance. Above all, it earnestly seeks the public's approval, for this one can't reach the people with a gun. People's opinion is like an infant. We must glue our hearts with them with the softness of love and affection and give up pride to win their hearts. It would help if you served them. One must remember the truth that violence always gives birth to violence, love to love, and light to light.

Arun again says, "We fight and will be fighting for the innocent people who are victimized and exploited daily in their lives by the rich and the hegemonic groups in power."

Satya again warns Arun, "Have you ever met your S.I.F.O. Chief? Have you ever understood where you get food, ammunition, and explosives? Or have you ever been given any chance to know all this? But why? Why are they so sympathetic to our country? Staying in foreign lands, they achieve their objectives using the people of this country. They never respect your aims."

Furthermore, Satya Sanatan adds, "Don't think murdering a commoner is an adventurous work. If you want to prove that you and your organization are more powerful and above the law and the government, you are mistaken. You will be mean if you want to take revenge.

You are afraid of the society. You have lost your courage to face the reality of life. Your future has terrified you so much that you are ready to bloodstain your present."

What your one lakh S.I.F.O. fighters do daily must be corrected.

But at the end of the play, Doctor Satya Sanatan and Alok have been released from the camp. The play has a strong message about how Gandhism wins over Terrorism or Extremism.

While translating the Odia play of the playwright into English, the rules of equivalence and the rules of faithfulness between the Odia language and the target language English are paid due attention. I came across some natural shifts. Some deictic expressions of the Odia language are retained in the target language English while translating.

I want to thank the playwright Dilliswar Moharana for believing in me to translate his Odia play *Varta* into English here. I would also like to thank Prof. Narayan Sahoo for helping me select the text for the English rendition.

I convey my heartfelt gratitude to Satya Pattanaik, the director of Black Eagle Books, U.S.A., and Sri Ashok Parida of the publishing house for their kind consent and timely action in publishing the work of art on time.

**Sanjeet Kumar Das**

# Dramatis Personae

| | | |
|---|---|---|
| Doctor Satyasanatana | : | A Senior Social Worker, Doctor and Writer |
| Arun | : | Highly Educated Young Man |
| Commander | : | An area Commander of the Extremist Group |
| Bul | : | Young Extremist |
| Paramapriya | : | A senior Politician and Chief Minister of the State |
| Anadi | : | An associate of Paramapriya and later the Minister of Culture |
| Danny | : | Close relative of Anadi and Paramapriya |
| Kulu | : | Young Contractor |
| Suresh | : | Arun's friend and an Extremist |
| Sugreeva | : | An Elderly Freedom Fighter |
| Nana | : | Cook of the Extremists' Residence |
| Mangaraj | : | Senior Journalist |
| Gautam | : | Police Officer |
| Priyanatha | : | Constable |
| Alok | : | A boy sheltering with the Extremists |
| Surabhi | : | Arun's Beloved |

## SCENE-I

[A series of past incidents]
[Two circles of light are on two sides of the stage. Arun is in one circle, while Surabhi is in another circle. Through dialogues, they respond to each other. They deliver dialogues in the style of writing letters. After the dialogue ends in one circle and the light of that circle is off, the other circle is on. The circle where Arun stands is lit with red light, while Surabhi's circle is coloured blue. The lights will symbolize pain and love for the two in circles.]

Surabhi : Arun Bhai, you told me to come to the village after the examination. It has already been six months since your M.A. results were published. Neither have you come, nor have you responded to any of my letters.

Arun : Believe me, Surabhi. I am interested in visiting my native place and seeing you all. But, before your father, I am ashamed to show my face. I couldn't arrange a job, though I stood First Class First in the M. A. programme.

Surabhi : My Dad is repeatedly asking about you. He complains that you are not coming at all to the village after your parents' death.

Arun : When I remember my village, before my

| | | |
|---|---|---|
| | | eyes are dancing the two doleful eyes of my older father. Moving to the court for eleven years, he couldn't retrieve our piece of ancestral land and breathed his last. |
| Surabhi | : | Yes, the touter Dhani Mohanty bribed the Officers and clerks so that we could not get that land, though we won the case. My father has been sick for the last few days. Yesterday evening, he called me and said, at any moment, I may pass away. I am interested in witnessing your marriage. |
| Arun | : | I will go to see Uncle at my convenience. This month I have many interviews. Attending them, I will certainly go. |
| Surabhi | : | In your last letter, you mentioned that you had to face an interview for the lecturer post at the University. What was your result? |
| Arun | : | I am facing interviews, but others are getting jobs. The Vice-Chancellor of the University conducted the interview. He was happy to see my testimonials and performance in the interview. I hope for the appointment letter. Please, wait for one more month. |
| Surabhi | : | It has already been four months, though you promised I would come in one month. Neither do you turn up nor do you reply to me. |
| Arun | : | (He shows the writing style in space, then acts like tearing the letter.) |

| Surabhi | : | Yesterday, I received an appointment letter from our M. E. School, Patna, as a teacher. I initially planned to write a letter to you mentioning this good news, but I thought it would be useless later. Two of my earlier letters have been returned to me, though I have sent them to the address you have given me. What has happened to you? Have I been a stranger to you that you can't convey everything? |

[Surabhi's eyes are welled up with tears. The stage lights are off.]

## SCENE-II

[It's the Government Quarters of the Minister Paramapriya. Anadisundar repeatedly dials someone inside the corridor of the quarters. Danny and Kulu are standing near him. Anadisundar is chewing betel. Arun enters. Anadi gets irritated after having seen Arun.]

| Anadi | : | Hello...hello...is it Superintending Engineer's office? Hello...hello...hello... no response.<br>[Arun enters.] |
| Arun | : | (To Arun Babu) Sir, Namaskar... |
| Anadi | : | (Shut up.) Danny Babu, this telephone line won't help us work for politics here. I am trying to ring up for half an hour... no chance... |
| Arun | : | Sir, can you help me meet the Minister? |
| Anadi | : | (Shut up.) Hello...hello... |

| | | |
|---|---|---|
| Danny | : | Anadi Babu, book a call instead of trying here through this S.T.D. call. If you get the first chance, we will talk. |
| Anadi | : | Danny Babu, using a mobile is not safe for us. There is clear instruction from the minister to use S.T.D.; otherwise, there is the possibility of our call being recorded. |
| Arun | : | Sir, please send this chit to the Honorable Minister. |
| Anadi | : | I observe you won't allow us to work here. This is the Minister's residential quarters' internal verandah. |
| Arun | : | Others are coming…I have come. |
| Anadi | : | Go to that side. Please talk to the P.A. On this side, nobody is allowed except Party Members. |
| Arun | : | I went to the Secretariat; they told me to meet him at his 'Residence'. I met the P.A.; he sent me to you. You are telling me to go that side. |
| Anadi | : | (Shut up) Hello…Sir…are you Superintending Engineer speaking? Namaskar Sir! I am calling from the Honorable Minister of Education's Residence. Hello…Our people, Danny and Kulu, have applied for the Tender for the bridge construction work. The Minister wants them to get the Tender. Hello…Danny Babu's name? What's your good name, Danny Babu? |
| Danny | : | Daniel Nayak. |
| Anadi | : | Daniel Nayak, Sir. He is the son of Nayak Babu, our D.I.G. Kulu Babu's name is |

|  |  |
|---|---|
|  | Manmath Patnaik, our M. P. Patnaik Babu's brother-in-law. Please see that they should get the tender at any cost. If you deny it, you can talk to the Chief of Engineers. Hello… (To Atun) … Have I not told you to go to that side? hello… hello…shit…again cut off… |
| Kulu | : Anadi Babu, he must have kept the receiver. He won't receive bribes or listen to others. |
| Danny | : What shall we do now, Anadi Babu? Can we get the Work Order in your presence? |
| Anadi | : Please, have patience. I must chalk out a plan to bring the S. E. to the track. (To Arun) why don't you understand? The Minister is on an evening walk on his lawn. A journalist is taking his interview there. Well, Danny Babu, Kulu Babu… Let's go to that side. This person won't allow us to work here. |

[Danny and Kulu enter inside after Anadi Babu. While Arun enters with them, Kulu talks to him in exasperation…]

| Kulu | : Hey, Babu, why are you disturbing us? The Minister is on that side. Go there to meet him. Why are you coming after us? [Arun starts to say something to Kulu, but the stage lights are off.] |

## SCENE-III

[Minister Paramapriya Patnaik is on the evening walk on the lawn of his residence. A journalist takes his interview holding a tape recorder. A senior journalist, the grey-haired ...his lousy habit of shaking his head is marked intermittently.]

Paramapriya : There is an ocean of difference between the erstwhile politics and today's politics. I have met many people from the Secretariat about their issues; now you can see that many have gathered here.

Mangaraj : Right! You are right!! People now have been more conscious and reactive than earlier. Sir, this is a good sign for the country.

Parama : No, not all. They have become lazy and lethargic in their lifestyle. They are making crowds before the people's representatives without solving their issues.

Mangaraj : Right! You are the senior Minister of the ruling party. You control the Government's Departments of Education, Forest, and Revenue. The commitments your party has promised in the political manifesto have yet to be executed.

Parama : Some are fulfilled, some are not. Some more we are planning.

Mangaraj : Then, what have you already fulfilled?

Parama : For example, our party has declared that the people will get rice in two rupees per

|  |  |
|---|---|
|  | kilogram. They are now getting. |
| Mangaraj | : Right, but out of that one, 1 kg rice, 600-gram pebbles or broken pieces of stones. |
| Parama | : This doesn't seem right. The opposite parties are making this an issue. We have formed an Inquiry Commission to investigate the matter. |
| Mangaraj | : Then, your commission is formed for the inquiry of 600 grams of pebbles in one kg of rice; otherwise, what's the need for commission formation? Sir, can you deny how people are dying of starvation occasionally? |
| Parama | : No, never. Our storehouses are full of rice, wheat, and cereals. There is no question of death by starvation. |
| Mangaraj | : But people die every day. The news gets published in the newspapers. |
| Parama | : These are your works. You people are publishing this saying the case of starvation, though some of them die for their old age and some of their diseases. Opposing this, we are denying the information. |
| Mangaraj | : Sir, your party has committed to providing more jobs for the unemployed youths. But this matter is still in progress, though you have run the Government for the last two years. |
| Parama | : Our Chief Minister himself has planned a budget for this. Have faith in us. It will be executed shortly. |
| Mangaraj | : It is said, "Unless that plan is worked |

|   |   |
|---|---|
| | out, one should not believe the persons whose initial letters are started with English 'P'." |
| Parama | : What are those Ps? |
| Mangaraj | : They are – Police, Pleader, Prostitute and Politician. People generally think that their promises can't be believed in so easily. |
| Parama | : Politicians can say so, but we are not the statesmen. |
| Mangaraj | : I don't see any difference between the politicians and the statesmen. |
| Parama | : There is a difference between them. A politician always thinks of the next Election, while a statesman thinks of the next Generation. |
| Mangaraj | : Politicians and statesmen are all the 'leaders' in the commoner's language. The leaders represent a 'a group', not an individual. They are of the same cadre, whether of the ruling or opposition party. Wine in all bottles remains the same. |
| Parama | : No, I can't accept this. Our party is above all this. You may go now. |
| Mangaraj | : One more query, Sir. Your party has assured the public of the removal of bad days. Your party hasn't taken any initiative so far for that. |
| Parama | : No…no…Our party leader is not the hero of the Hindi film who can change everything within three hours. Everything will be set right gradually. Monkey has evolved into man gradually; |

|  |  |
|---|---|
|  | the earth from the gaseous state has slowly come to this solid state. After that, we find trees, fish, man and earth. Everything happens slowly on this earth. [Anadisundar enters holding a cordless phone in hand.] |
| Anadi | : Sir, Doctor Satysanatan's call. |
| Parama | : Well, Mangaraj Babu, you can go now. I have some other engagements. |
| Mangaraj | : Right, Sir. Thank you. Good day, Sir! |

[Mangaraj Babu leaves. Paramapriya talks over the phone, taking the receiver from Anadi Babu. Anadi enters inside. The doctor talks to him from the other side of the stage. That place is lit.]

| Satya | : Hello...Namaskar, Bhai...How did you remember me suddenly? |
|---|---|
| Parama | : It's not sudden, my brother. My P.A. is trying to contact you consistently, but you have picked up the call now. |
| Satya | : Do you have any work with me? Had you told me, I would have gone to meet you. |
| Parama | : No need to meet me again. You can't be appointed the Vice-Chancellor of the University...You have stated this in the newspapers. This means you have slapped me. |
| Satya | : What do you mean? |
| Parama | : I have worked hard before the Chief Minister and the Honorable Governor for the post of Vice-Chancellor for you. But |

|          |   |                                                                                                                                                                                                                                                                                                                                                                                                                                                                                                 |
|----------|---|---|
|          |   | you have insulted me by refusing this post. |
| Satya    | : | (Smiling) If I have insulted you, please forgive me. I am not so educated for that post…there is a need for an educationist. |
| Parama   | : | Educationist? Who is a better educationist than you here in this state? You have studied Medical Sciences in England, America, and many other countries. You have been working there day and night, opening schools and hospitals free of cost for the tribal children. You have published so many books on social reformation. Brother, your life itself is a university. Please accept this post to show the right direction to the youth of the state. |
| Satya    | : | No, Brother…Unless what I have started here in the Ashram is over, I can't go anywhere. |
| Parama   | : | I know this rightly…You have promised to insult a friend like me. If you change your mind anytime, you will bring it to my knowledge. Yes…At least you give some proposals for your orphanage and hospital. If I don't help you as a friend, what's the use of my ministerial post/position here? |
| Satya    | : | It is decided that these will be built without Government or Charitable Organization's assistance…You know it very well, my brother, Paramapriaya. In case of any emergency, I will certainly |

|  |  |  |
|---|---|---|
|  |  | contact you. I know you will never hesitate to help a friend like me. Okay, thank you, Brother. |
| Parama | : | Right…Who cares whether one helps others or not but let our friendship live long. |
| Satya | : | (Chorus) Namaskar! |
| Parama | : | [Both of them laugh. The light of the zone where Doctor Satya Sanatana stands is off. Anadi, Danny, and Lulu enter. Paramapriya gives the receiver to Anadi Babu.] |
| Parama | : | Have you solved their problem? |
| Anadi | : | I have talked to the Superintending Engineer about this. Here, Danny and Kulu say nothing happens in his hand. You must report this to the Chief Engineer. |
| Danny | : | Yes, Uncle. The Minister of the Finance Department has gone abroad. If you have a word with the chief Engineer, we will retain the Tender. |
| Parama | : | All right, go to the P.A. and tell him to ring up the Chief Engineer and say he will meet me tonight.<br>[Danny and Kulu return.]<br>Anadisundar… |
| Anadi | : | Sir!! |
| Parama | : | What's the progress/status of your work? |
| Anadi | : | Eighty-seven M.L.A.s have already signed. We have arranged a party for those five M.L.A.s of the Scheduled Tribes on the following Sunday. Danny and Kulu Babu will bear all this. |

| | | |
|---|---|---|
| Parama | : | We must do all this cautiously. The Chief Minister should not doubt that I am the leader of the dissatisfied/annoyed group. All the arrangements will be over...All will resign simultaneously. |
| Anadi | : | No need to explain, Sir. When we have decided to step up, we will...if we relax ourselves anywhere, we will be thrown down in this 'tail-holding' business. I know this very well. |
| Parama | : | What do you mean by saying 'Tail-holding' business? |
| Anadi | : | Sir, 'Politics' is a tail-holding business. All say here everybody steps up holding the tail of others. |
| Parama | : | What does this mean? |
| Anadi | : | Sir, you first became the Sarpanch... Holding your tail, I became the Control Retailer. With the support from others, you became the Block chairman, and I became Sarpanch. After that, you became the M. L. A., while I became the Block Chairman. Now you are trying to break the Ministry to become the Chief Minister; how can I stay aloof, Sir? I won't leave you. At least a Minister of the State I can be. |

[Arun enters suddenly. Paramapriya and Anadi stop laughing.]

| | | |
|---|---|---|
| Arun | : | Namaskar, Sir! |
| Parama | : | Have I seen you at the Secretariat? |
| Arun | : | Yes, I couldn't meet you even three hours |

| | | after I submitted my chit. Later, I wanted to meet you on the road. You returned telling me to meet you tomorrow. |
|---|---|---|
| Parama | : | Then, why have you come here today? You can leave now. Tomorrow, you will meet me in the morning. |
| Arun | : | No, Sir. Like you, I don't have a residence, car or motorbike in this capital. How can I come to meet you? Having come to meet you, I have been sleeping in the 'Waiting Hall' of the station for the last three days. |
| Parama | : | All right, please tell me your problem. |
| Arun | : | I am Arun Mohapatra. I faced an interview for the lecturer post at the university. Though I performed well in the interview, someone else was issued the appointment letter. |
| Parama | : | How can I help you here? Please go to meet the Vice Chancellor regarding this. |
| Arun | : | Yes, I am returning from him. You are the Minister of the Department of Higher Education. I have come to you for justice. |
| Parama | : | All right…then, how did you know your performance was the best in the interview? |
| Arun | : | I know all the candidates who came to face the interview. None of them can perform better than me. |
| Parama | : | Sometimes overconfidence puts you in trouble. One better than you in Academic Career might be issued the appointment letter. |
| Arun | : | Had it been so, I would not have raised |

|  |  |
|---|---|
| | my voice. But the letter is issued to one who, throughout his life, had been a backbencher in the classroom. Though his career could have been better, he managed to secure First Class in the M. A. programme. He can't perform better than me in the interview. |
| Parama : | All right…Give a representation to me. |
| Arun : | (Bringing out a pen from his pocket) Everything is written here. |
| Parama : | (Reading) What's this nonsense? Because of me, you have been deprived of this job. |
| Arun : | Yes. As per your recommendation, someone else has been appointed in my place. |
| Parama : | Are you mad? Why can I order like that? |
| Arun : | You have ordered that. |
| Parama : | Do you challenge me? |
| Arun : | No sir, I have come here to listen to you. |
| Parama : | Complaining to me, you have come to hear me. |
| Arun : | Yes, I lost my parents some days ago. Unable to meet the expenditures of my studies, I arranged students' tuition from morning to evening and spent sleepless nights in starvation. I have secured the highest position at the university. Sir, you couldn't think of me before shattering the hopes of my entire life. |
| Parama : | You are talking nonsense. A political enemy of mine might have plotted this conspiracy against me for rivalry. I |

| | | |
|---|---|---|
| | | did not know that guy, nor did I order anyone to give him the job. You can go now. |
| Anadi | : | You can go now. Don't shout here. Sir has denied you. Please go now. |
| Arun | : | I have yet to cover a twenty-kilometer-long road to return. Please let me know whether you know that guy or not. |
| Parama | : | Have I to obey all this forcibly? |
| Arun | : | Yes, that guy is your concubine's son. He is our village social worker Shanti Das's son. |
| Paramapriya | : | You scoundrel… [Paramapriya raises his hand to slap Arun. Holding that hand, Arun tries to get hold of the Minister's collar. When they are fighting, Danny and Kulu intervene and separate Arun. He again moves ahead to assault Parampriya. Danny and Kulu threw him down. Arun roars like a fierce lion. Anadi tries to contact the Police Station through the phone.] |
| Arun | : | I will take revenge on you one day. I will spell out everything, crying out, Bastard Paramapriya. I will shoot you, Bastard. |
| Anadi | : | Hello…Police Station…Hello…Capital Police Station…Hello… |

# SCENE-IV

[It's the Capital Police Station. The 'Bande Mataram' song is played at a distance from the radio. Wearing the police dress and holding a bell in one hand and a stand to place burning incense in the other, the Constable enters chanting the *mantras* before the photos of the deities hung on the wall.]

Priyanath : "om nāgendra hārāya trilochanāya…"

[When the Constable chants *mantras,* the Police Station in charge, Gautam Orama Das, have reached there. Priyanath, in the meanwhile, salutes hurriedly and worships the deity chanting *mantras.*]

Gautam : You mean 'Constable'. Who has told you to do all this inside the Police Station?

Priya : Hari Om! Who will say? Sir, our earlier officers have continued this tradition of waving incense sticks before the deities every morning and evening.

Gautam : What nonsense? Was an erstwhile Police Officer telling you to worship the deities inside the Police Station?

Priya : Yes, Sir. The erstwhile Police Officer Balmukunda Balabanta Ray Samanta was a devout religious person. He didn't see any difference between *Hari Om* Temple and Police Station.

Gautam : The Temple is a religious institution, whereas the Police Station is a public office. These two can't be identical.

Priyanath : *Hari Om* may not be identical to the Police Station, but the activities are equal.

|   |   |
|---|---|
| | The way one can't see God entering the temple without *Dakshina* (Offerings), similarly no entry to the Police Station without *Hari Om*... |
| Gautam | : Shut up! Worshipping inside the secular state's public office...these are all the bogus thoughts. From today onwards, I order this to stop. Do you understand? "Do as you are directed" Balmukunda Balabanta Ray Samanta's order was executed. Now he is no longer here. You have joined here in his place. I will obey your command. |
| Gautam | : Not only that, but you will also take away all the photos from the walls tomorrow. Gautam Oram Das is a secular police officer. He is truly Indian in spirit. He has been trained on how to respect all religions. |
| Priyanath | : Hari Om, I couldn't understand!! |
| Gautam | : My father was a devout Hindu. His surname was 'Das'. My mother was a tribal Christian whose surname was 'Oram'. I have taken the surnames of my father and mother together. Thus, my name is Gautam Oram Das. People call me in short form G. O. D. Before me, all religions are equal. I need to remember your name. |
| Priyanath | : Hari Om Priyanath Pati. This is your third day. How can you remember my name so quickly? |
| Gautam | : Priyanath Pati!! It isn't easy to utter. |

| | | |
|---|---|---|
| Priyanath | : | Hari Om! You can't call me either from the beginning, middle, or end. Our lady Constables can't call me out of shame. |
| Gautam | : | "Lady Constables can't call..." What do you mean by saying that? |
| Priyanath | : | Sir, my name is Priyanath Pati. They say...they can't call 'Priya', they can't call 'Nath', or they can't call 'Pati'.<br>[Gautam is about to laugh but controls himself.] |
| Gautam | : | Yes, you are right. I alert you from the outset that you must be vigilant while working with me. Gautam Oram Das... Before G.O.D., he will be happy if all execute their duties rightly. He will chase others like a dog if he sees any deviation from the duties. Do you understand? |
| Priyanath | : | Hari Om, right! I agree with you entirely. If the word 'God' is reversed, it becomes 'Dog'. "Duty is God/ work is worship". This is also written in *The Bhagavata Gita*. |
| Gautam | : | Yes, duty is first. So, be careful. You will work as per my order on the spot. That's why you must always be ready, Shambunath. |
| Priyanath | : | Hari Om, I am not Shambunath, I am Priyanath. |
| Gautam | : | Yes, Priyanath! Is the phrase 'Hari Om' before your name 'the salutation'? |
| Priyanath | : | This is 'Gurumantra', Sir. My wife and I surrendered before a 'Guru' in Kashi, expecting a son after having been blessed with eleven daughters. Gurudev |

|  |  |  |
|---|---|---|
|  |  | consecrated us with the 'Hari Om' mantra, and then we are fortunately, by God's grace, blessed with our twelfth child, a son. |
| Gautam | : | What's the need for using the phrase 'Hari Om' before every word? |
| Priyanath | : | Every day, there is an order from the Guru to chant one lakh time *mantra*, Sir. I need help to do so 24x7 police duty. So, I am adjusting this in the conversation. |
| Gautam | : | No, this is not good practice on police job. You must give up this habit or resign from the post. It's my order. |
| Priyanath | : | (Unhappily) I was trying to be an ideal of the Police department, virtuous by nature. When you have ordered, I must obey it. I have been habituated with the 'Hari Om' for several days. By chance, if it comes out of my mouth, you will forgive me. You will pardon me. |

[Bringing out the handkerchief from his pocket, he tears apart the 'rosary' and removes the sandalwood drops from his forehead.]

| Gautam | : | Bravo! Hearing the order from the Officer, you have executed immediately. I am pleased with you now. The government works will run smoothly if we coordinate one another. |
|---|---|---|
| Priyanath | : | Yes, Sir. When a dispassionate, non-violent Constable like me is with a dutiful secular police officer like you, the Police Station will be fortunate enough to march ahead, Sir. |

| | | |
|---|---|---|
| Gautam | : | Yes, you will help me. I will also help you. Otherwise, it will be tough to govern the Capital Police station. All from S.P. to IG will seek our help. If we don't work together, we can't satisfy them. |
| Priyanath | : | One 100 per cent, Sir. They need help understanding our poor officers. Our department has yet to be allotted the cement, iron rod, or teak forest where we can manage to sell them. We must manage ourselves depending upon the offensive thugs, thieves, etc., in the capital city… again these people are, however, linked with the ministers. These ministers will receive a percentage first of what they will earn from the market. Who will ask this Police Station? |
| Gautam | : | Where's the Sound now? |
| Priyanath | : | Sir, the boy who created a nuisance yesterday becomes violent occasionally. |
| Gautam | : | He was severely beaten last night. He is still roaring in the other room. All right! Do you know him before? |
| Priyanath | : | No, So. He is not from this capital. Please forward him to court without any further delay. Nobody will come to take him on bail. You can't get a single penny from his pocket. |
| Gautam | : | What do you mean? |
| Priyanath | : | After having been thrashed yesterday, he became senseless. I found seven rupees only from him. He is so miserly that he doesn't wear a wristwatch or a ring on |

The Message | 37

|            |   |                                                                                                                                                                                                                                                                                                                                           |
|------------|---|-------------------------------------------------------------------------------------------------------------------------------------------------------------------------------------------------------------------------------------------------------------------------------------------------------------------------------------------|
|            |   | his fingers. What's the benefit of keeping him here?                                                                                                                                                                                                                                                                                      |
| Gautam     | : | Go to the Junior Officer and tell him to prepare his documents to forward him to the court.                                                                                                                                                                                                                                               |
| Priyanath  | : | If we don't send this useless fellow to the court, our entire day will go in vain. We have been transferred to the Capital police station and are spending a lot. If we get people like him, we can't show our faces to our wives in the evening. Yes, I will prepare his documents to forward him to court. |

[Priyanath leaves. A message is heard in the wireless. Gautam talks to Someone in one corner of the room.]

| Wireless | : | Capital Police Station…Capital Police Station |
| Gautam | : | Hello…Yes, Officer-in-charge on the line…over. |
| Wireless | : | (From the machine) Note down message…from…I.G. Some "S.I.F.O." extremists have entered the capital. You are directed to be ready to go on 'Operation' at any moment…Over. [The sound of a vehicle is outside. Anandisundar enters.] |
| Anadi | : | Are you the Officer-in-charge, Gautam Babu? |
| Gautam | : | Yes, what happened? |
| Anadi | : | My name is Anadisundar Barik. Sir, please call the guy whom your police |

|  |  |
|---|---|
| | Officer arrested last night. I want to talk to him. |
| Gautam | : We are busy forwarding him to court. He is in the next room. |
| Anadi | : All right. Please keep him here for three to four more days. Don't forward him to court now? |
| Gautam | : No, we can't do that. We can't keep anybody here for more than twenty-four hours. |
| Anadi | : Anyhow, you must do so. The Minister wants this. |
| Gautam | : If the Minister wants, it won't be good. |
| Anadi | : Don't use your mind to decide what's good or not. That will be good if you execute what is said. |
| Gautam | : But, in the F.I.R., it is written that he wanted to murder the Minister. |
| Anadi | : He wanted. Had he murdered the Minister? (He speaks slowly.) The Minister wants this not to be an issue. Sir, let him be in your custody only. You will release him when he is brought under your complete control. |
| Gautam | : Then, withdraw the F. I. R. you have submitted here, or else it will be a problem. |
| Anadi | : Oh! As per the instructions of the Minister, I communicated this to you. That's all from my side. You will understand what to do next. |
| Gautam | : But this is very critical… |
| Anadi | : (Smiling) You have recently joined |

|         |   the office. Everything runs here as per the ministers' order. Those who work here either are the Minister's people or become gradually. If you want to change your decision, you won't inform through a phone call. You will come straight to the Minister's residence.<br>[Driver, start the vehicle.]<br>[Anadi leaves. Later, the Jeep starts and disappears.] |
|---------|---|
| Gautam  | : It's a bogus place. Oh, shit! |

[Out of anger, Gautam beats his hand with a baton. By mistake, it touched his thumb, and he experienced pain. He starts to suck that thumb suddenly.] [Light off]

# SCENE-V

[It's the house of Suresh Singh. Nothing else is found except two wooden chairs. This news is heard in the darkness.]

| News | : It is known from our special correspondent that Save India Fighter Organization (S.I.F.O.) extremists murdered the engineer Durga Prasad Mishra of the Sundar Valley Project and his wife last night. The entire country condemned the bank loot and the murder of the engineer's family members made by the extremists. The Opposition Party blamed the government for its futile action and silence against the S.I.F.O. group. |
|---|---|

[The stage lights are on. The Commander of the extremist group is seen reading the news. He is waiting for someone to tell us. Bul comes in.]

| | | |
|---|---|---|
| Commander | : | (Through body language) What happened? |
| Bul | : | I don't know anything, Commander, but I smell a rat. |
| Commander | : | He should return by 1.00 A.M. tonight. It's 3 O'clock. |
| Bul | : | Don't worry. He will return after success. |
| Commander | : | He has taken my bike. He should be on time. Is there anything wrong? I am getting upset now because of his delay in returning. |
| | | [Sound of knocking on the door] |
| Bul | : | Now he has come, Commander… |
| Commander | : | Don't be silly, Bul. Don't open the door like a fool. Had Suresh come, there would have been the Sound of the motorbike. |
| Bul | : | Who can come here other than Suresh to us at midnight to come, Commander? |
| Commander | : | You go first to the rooftop and watch. If you see any stranger or Police Officer, you will hint at me. I am switching off the light. |

[Someone is knocking on the door. The room lights are switched off. Bul moves in a different direction, and the Commander comes to a position while the door is knocked on. Arun enters the room suddenly. The Commander brings him to his control from the back side. Arun falls to the ground. Bul runs to them.]

| | | |
|---|---|---|
| Commander | : | Don't move. Stay there. But how did the door get opened? Let him be shut well in the room. |

[Bul steps out and shuts the door from outside. Who are you? Why are you here late at night?]

| | | |
|---|---|---|
| Arun | : | (He is so tired that he can't say anything.) You…who are you here? |
| Commander | : | Shut up! How many are there with you? (Bul returns.) (Bul do check him now. Bul checks him.) |
| Bul | : | Is there anybody with you? Why can't you say? |
| Arun | : | Nobody has come with me. I have come running here for my life in danger. |
| Commander | : | Why here? Why have you come running to this house? Rascal!! You must be the informer to the Police. (He is beating.) |
| Arun | : | No, this is my friend Suresh's house. The 'Agnibana' Magazine's Signboard is installed here. |
| Commander | : | Yes, it was *Agnibana* Magazine's Office before. Now, it is not. |
| Bul | : | This bastard is hiding something from us. We will shoot him. (He is beating.) |
| Arun | : | I am Arun Mohapatra, a friend of Suresh. I have escaped from Police Custody. Please give me a glass of water. I am very thirsty. |
| Commander | : | Bul, take him to that room. After Suresh returns, he will understand his case. |
| Bul | : | Let's move…we will drink water there… let's move. |

[Bul pushes Arun into the room. Suresh's voice is heard outside.]

Suresh : Commander...Commander...

[Commander opens the door, and Suresh comes in.]

*Salam* (I salute you!) Commander!! The fighter Suresh has returned after achieving the target.

Commander : Have you taken wine again?

Suresh : As directed, I have neutralized the Police Officer and two constables there. I have murdered three giants/demons from this country. At this auspicious moment, I couldn't control myself without taking liquor, Commander.

[Bul comes from inside.]

Commander : All right. Take a rest, give me the bike's key. We are going to the camp.

Suresh : No, Commander, no. I won't allow you to go. You have taken a rest at my home. I won't let you go without pleasing you.

Commander : Suresh, you are forgetting your responsibility for your inebriated state. I am afraid that you will be a problem for the 'S.I.F.O.' one day since you work very carelessly. You have returned murdering all in one Police Station...At any moment, the Police may reach here.

Suresh : Commander, I have accomplished my task. You are angry with me unnecessarily. I am fully, all right.

Commander : All right...I am going to the camp. One of your friends has come here. If he seems suspicious, it is your responsibility to

| | | |
|---|---|---|
| | | finish him. I will see you tomorrow evening. Bul! You come! |
| | | [Commander and Bul leave the place.] |
| Suresh | : | Who is my friend sheltering here? Where is he? Suresh Singh's friend…Hah…hah…hah. Suresh's friend is this gun (He kisses the gun. Arun stands there.) Oh, you are my friend. I don't have any friends like you. Speak the truth…why don't you say? (Slapping him) who are you? …who are you? |
| Arun | : | Suresh…What are you saying? Can't you recognize me? I am Arun, whom you were calling 'Lion'. |

[Arun shakes Suresh's body. Suresh becomes conscious. He looks at Arun as a fool and cries like an infant.]

| | | |
|---|---|---|
| | | What is all this, Suresh? Please stop it. |
| Suresh | : | Please forgive me, Lion! I have been mad (Embracing him). Forgive me. |
| Arun | : | What has happened to you, Suresh? I can't understand one who denied having a betel leaf. Where are your magazines, press, poems, and new socialistic ideology? Where are they? |
| Suresh | : | Lion, these are all bogus thoughts. The revolution will come to this country not by pen but by the gun. Poems, speech…, and intellectual discussions are all useless. Those rascals drink human blood in broad daylight…likewise, we must celebrate the 'Festival of Colours' with their blood. Are you listening to me, |

|  |  |
|---|---|
| | Lion…They have murdered my parents. They have burnt my Magazine Press. My father was writing an 'Editorial' sitting there. My mother was passing the cup of tea to him here. They have ruined me, Lion! Nobody can do any harm to them… Nobody…they are rich people…they are ruling from the centre. I will take revenge upon them. |
| Arun | : Then you have joined the 'Extremists Group'. |
| Suresh | : This is not the 'Extremist Group', but the 'Insurgent Group'. They call the "Save India Fighter's Organization" (S.I.F.O.) a terrorist group. It's wrong. This 'S.I.F.O.' is a radical institution to bring about a change after removing the half-capitalist and half-fascist ruling class from power. Our slogan is 'Blood for the Country.' |

[Commander and Bul come suddenly.]

| | |
|---|---|
| Commander | : Suresh, I have returned patrolling two police vans at the front square. They may cordon off this area. We must leave this place. |
| Bul | : Yes, Suresh Bhaiya, be ready to leave. |
| Suresh | : Brother Lion…I can't hear you…Please forgive me. |
| Commander | : Quick. Save time. We must take him with us. |
| Suresh | : Arun is my friend. It won't be right to take him with us. |
| Commander | : He may be your friend, but he is not S.I.F.O.'s friend. We can't leave him like |

| | | |
|---|---|---|
| | | this. |
| Suresh | : | But…Why will he go with us? |
| Arun | : | I am ready to go with you, Suresh. I am prepared to face any test that your Commander wants. |

[Police officer announces using the microphone outside.]

| | | |
|---|---|---|
| Announcement: | | Your attention, please. All are informed here to come out of your houses because some S.I.F.O. extremists are sheltering here. All step out of the homes with your hands up. |
| Commander | : | The Police have started their combing operation. Switch off all the lights at our house. All come to the rooftop through the backside. Follow me; we can walk around responding to them rightly… Come on. |

[Police siren nears them—Police Officer orders to besiege that house. Commander Bul and Suresh take their positions. The siren becomes louder. The Commander throws a bomb towards the Police. After the sound of explosion, the stage lights are off.]

## SCENE-VI

[It's Surabhi's house. Surabhi's father, Sugreeva Nayak, is reading a newspaper. Different slogans of vote campaigning are heard at a distance through a microphone.]

| | | |
|---|---|---|
| Vote Campaigning | : | [Our leader, your leader, everybody's leader is Paramapriya…Live long (Thrice) Our symbol, your symbol, |

everybody's symbol is 'Sun Symbol'... Live long (thrice). Danny and Kulu are taking responsibility for all this.]

Surabhi : (She comes holding a cup of tea.)
Sugreeva : Have you received any letter from Arun?
Surabhi : No, Dad. We have not received any information about him for the last six months. Two of my letters have been returned to me from his earlier address.
Sugreeva : After his parents pass away, he is helpless. He is struggling hard alone in the battle of life. He must be searching for a job.

[From the microphone is heard, Brothers! After a while, our beloved leader, Minister Paramapriya Patnaik, will arrive here. Please be seated peacefully. A video show will be shown after the meeting is over.]

Surabhi : To the 'Field where congregation of idols' we watch every year, the President of Jana Sevak Party and M. L. A candidate Anadi Babu is coming.
Sugeeva : Has the breaker of other families, Anadi Babu, got the M. L. A. ticket? Do you know him? His house is twenty-one kilometres away from Nuagaon. He is a hypocrite, characterless person.
Surabhi : He is the right hand of Party President Paramapriya Patnaik. It is published in the newspapers that these two are responsible for the fall of the Government.
Sugreeva : "Like father, like son"...Anadi's father avails the "Freedom Fighter's Allowance". He was not a Freedom

Fighter...He stayed with others in the jail and informed the *Gora Sahibs* (the English/Britishers). A traitor of the country now receives a pension for the service to the country. His son is Anadi...He is going to be an M.L.A.

[Again, it is heard in the microphone, our leader Anadi Babu...Live long. After that...Brothers, our beloved leader, Sri Paramapriya Patnaik and M. L. A. candidate Anadi Babu have reached here.]

[Light off]

# SCENE-VII

[The light is shifted from Surabhi's family zone to the stage of the meeting place. Anadi Babu delivers a speech. Danny and Kuku are standing behind him.]

Anadi : Brothers! Uncles and Aunts!!! I convey to you all my regards. For the first time, I stand to contest as an M.L.A. candidate. The Member of Legislative Assembly candidates who won here earlier were the teachers and from the other Election Constituencies. They have not done any developmental work in this region. My village is twenty-five kilometers away from here in Nuagaon. Whatever development I have made in this region as the Block Chairman is uncountable. If I name it individually, others will think he is boasting. I have decided to build the

Bhogara River's bridge if you cast your votes and help me win the Election. For your village Goddess's sake, I promise that the bridge construction will be my priority. If I am unable to do so, you will then tell me.

[One from the audience says, "Will we get any chance to see you?" Then the people start laughing.]

Anadi : No, Sir; then you will arrange a meeting and rebuke me as much as you want.

[From the audience...We will tell you a dog. Anadi stammers, getting irritated in the audience's laughter.]

Anadi : Yes, If I don't build any bridge, you will call me by the dog's name, Sir. I don't have anything to say. Now, our most beloved leader, the founder of Jana Sevak Party Sri Paramapriya Patnaik, will speak on the microphone. He will help you understand how he took the leadership against the Government fall and how he formed the Jana Sevak Party. He will explain everything in detail. Thank you, all. Namaskar!!!

[While getting down from the stage, Anadi will fall. The audience will laugh at such a sight.]

[Light off]

# SCENE-VIII

[Surabhi's house is lit.]

Sugreeva : What a brilliant speech! Can you hear?

Surabhi : The Jana Sevak Party has distributed tickets among its members, and they are contesting Elections every place this year. They are spending money exorbitantly. The hooligans are campaigning for the candidates. They are terrifying the people in the villages. They will win.

Sugreeva : Our people are straightforward, my daughter. They are so quiet that they won't say anything, even if they are in danger.

Surabhi : Only the rascals and hypocrites take advantage of this.

Sugreeva : The lack of education! Gandhiji was protesting the British Education System. He said, 'The education system without moral lessons creates employability, but not human beings.'

[In front of Sugeeva's house, the 'Long Live' slogan is heard. Danny enters their building.]

Danny : Is Sugreeba uncle at home? Sir…please come.

[Anadi and Kulu enter.]

Sugreeva : How come you are at my home, suddenly?

Anadi : It's not sudden, Uncle. Many days before, we had already decided to come to your home to seek your blessing on behalf of the Jana Sevak Party.

[Anadi touches Sugreeva's feet for blessing.]

| | | |
|---|---|---|
| Sugreeva | : | What are all these? Why do you touch my feet? Surabhi, bring two chairs from that side. |
| Anadi | : | No, there is no need. Your compassion and blessings for us will be enough. |
| Sugreeva | : | Nowadays, our blessings won't help you win the Election; the people have learnt how to take their decisions and how to cast their votes. |
| Anadi | : | No, Uncle…it won't work if you say so. If you want, these fifty villages will cast their votes in favour of our Jana Sevak Party. |
| Sugreeva | : | This is your misconception. You must go and ask the people for their votes. You must convince them in your style. Nowadays, you appear only during the Election. |
| Anadi | : | Uncle, our Party can never do that. We have promised or taken oath to serve the people. |
| Danny | : | Please say 'Yes' to our Party and support our Party. Our members are here to hear from you. |
| Kulu | : | You need not say anything to anybody. You say 'Yes'. It is our responsibility to control the public. |
| Sugreeva | : | Who are you all, my sons? |
| Anadi | : | They are the Youth Group of the Jana Sevak Party. They are Danny Babu, and Kulu Babu. Very nice fellows! |

| | | |
|---|---|---|
| Sugreeva | : | I have heard that you are terrifying the people here. |
| | | [Anadi gets shocked.] |
| Anadi | : | Our Opposition Party has campaigned against us, Uncle. You don't believe all this. |
| Sugreeva | : | No party has come to meet me so far. I am telling you what I have heard from the people. |
| | | [Danny and Kulu are unhappy now.] |
| Danny | : | Let's move, Anadi Babu. We have another meeting in this village. If you give these wrinkled-skinned fellows a chance, they won't listen to you because they think of themselves as 'Mahatma Gandhi'. |
| Anadi | : | Danny Babu, you shouldn't say so to the uncle. |
| Kulu | : | How should we treat him? Please come. We know well how to win the Election. |
| | | [Danny and Kulu leave the place.] |
| Anadi | : | Danny Babu...Kulu Babu...Please, listen to me. These youngsters don't recognize you. I will come to you again. |

[Before Anadi leaves the place, he takes blessings by touching Sugreeva' feet. All the lights focus on Sugreeva's face. He is humiliated. Surabhi gets hold of him. The stage lights are off.]

# SCENE-IX

[Another day, Gandhiji's favourite hymn, *"Vaishnav Jana to tene kahiye,"* is heard outside Surabhi's house. Arun comes from outside. He covers his body with a shawl. Under the shawl, he has hidden an AK-47 rifle in a bag. Arun looks around there. Without anybody's knowledge, he carefully tries to hide the bag. No one is aware of the rifle that he has brought. After that, Surabhi enters.]

| | | |
|---|---|---|
| Surabhi | : | Who is here? Who are you searching for? My father is not at home. |
| Arun | : | Don't you recognize me, Surabhi? I am Arun. |
| Surabhi | : | Arun Bhai…you…I didn't expect you to reach here at this odd time. |
| Arun | : | When will Uncle return? |
| Surabhi | : | He has gone to meet the members of the Freedom Fighters' Council. He will return late at night. |
| Arun | : | How are you? |
| Surabhi | : | Forget about me. Can you first say where you were for so many days? Neither any information nor any letter was sent to us. |
| Arun | : | Will you question me like this or give me a glass of water? |
| Surabhi | : | (Getting hold of Arun's bag) Won't you remove your bag from your shoulder? Give that to me. Then go to the washroom. Could you give me that? |

[Surabhi extends her hand to him for the bag; Arun retracts his body from her.]

| | | |
|---|---|---|
| Arun | : | Hold on; I have come here in an emergency. I can stay here for a short time. |

[Surabhi's face colour changes for her self-pride.]

| | | |
|---|---|---|
| Surabhi | : | You have come here after a long time… how can you leave the place without meeting my father? |
| Arun | : | Some of my friends will reach here shortly. I must go with them. |
| Surabhi | : | Then, why did you come here? We have almost forgotten you. Please be here; I am coming with a glass of water. |

[Surabhi comes with a glass of water from inside.]

| | | |
|---|---|---|
| Arun | : | Try to understand me, Surabhi. I have not stayed anywhere permanently for the last few months. So, I couldn't provide you with any permanent address to write letters to me. I wander day and night for work. You can't understand that. |
| Surabhi | : | I can understand you well. One can't be with any love and affection if he deals with rifles and bullets. |
| Arun | : | How could you know, "I am with bullets and rifle?" (Checking his bag) Oh, what's this then. (He hides the bag well, so the gun won't be visible.) |
| Surabhi | : | You didn't allow me to touch your bag, but I could mark it well. Arun Bhai, what has happened to you? Why are you roaming with all these? |
| Arun | : | I have joined the revolutionary group 'S.I.F.O.'. The freedom of the country is lost and ruined. We have all taken an oath to safeguard this. |

| | | |
|---|---|---|
| Surabhi | : | Are you earning pleasure from killing hundreds of innocent people to save the country? Are you happy to do so? |
| Arun | : | Surabhi, this is not the question of happiness...I am executing my duties for the country. There is an ocean of difference between killing people for one's pride and killing for the formation of a healthy and prosperous society. By doing so, the dream of society can be brighter than it was before. |
| Surabhi | : | Is it possible to dream of a healthy society by plundering society? Is there no other way for that? |
| Arun | : | If all other ways are closed or blocked for an individual? |
| Surabhi | : | Then he becomes a murderer. Do you want to say this? |
| Arun | : | Who is here, the murderer? Whether we or the Government? We control a small group of people at gunpoint. But what about the so-called Capitalists of the country who adulterate the poisonous brunt mobil in the oil and make hundreds of people suffer forever? Are they not killing people by selling fake medicines despite their unwillingness? The Politicians and Bureaucrats help them. What are they doing? Are they not killers? |
| Surabhi | : | They may be the murderers. Can this country be reformed and safe after neutralizing them? |

| | | |
|---|---|---|
| Arun | : | We will find out the way for social transformation. We must stop their monopoly or autocracy by killing them. If we bring terror and menace into their minds, they will understand that some are here to punish them. Surabhi, is it not ideal to sacrifice one's life to protest the injustice prevalent in society or country? |
| Surabhi | : | Arun Bhai, this tiny head can't understand whether it is ideal or not. Life is yours… You have the right to use it as you want. Please be seated. I will at least arrange a light tiffin for you. |
| Arun | : | Stop it. I don't have time for that. I have come here to tell you one point only. |
| Surabhi | : | I have already understood what you want to tell me today. |
| Arun | : | You have not understood that. I want to make it clear to you today. |
| Surabhi | : | (Her voice gets choked.) Stop, Arun Bhai, you stop here. I request you not to say anything to me. I don't want to hear all those words from you. |
| Arun | : | Staying away from all kinds of emotions, I want to clear you all, though it is very tough to bear. |
| Surabhi | : | (Roaring suddenly) I have sworn to safeguard my country. There is no place for love, affection, or sympathy before such great work. You will need to remember the promise we made earlier for our marriage and to have kids. Haven't you come to say all these? |

| | | |
|---|---|---|
| Sugreeva | : | Surabhi...bring light to this side. [Surabhi comes with a torch.] |
| Arun | : | I am leaving the place on this way. Uncle should not know that I have visited here. |

[Surabhi sheds tears and accompanies her father; Arun escapes in another direction.]

| | | |
|---|---|---|
| Sugreeva | : | We will complete our work soon. They arranged for my stay there, but I denied it. I left the meeting after it was over. Hey...why aren't you saying anything?... What has happened to you? |
| Surabhi | : | No, Dad...nothing has happened to me. I am terrified in the early evening alone. Won't you have your dinner? |
| Sugreeva | : | No, I have had my food there... Please give me the newspaper so that I can glance over the issues. |

[Surabhi brings a newspaper from inside. Sugreeva starts reading it. A motorbike stops before their house suddenly. The stage is lit in the bike's light. When Surabhi proceeds in that direction, Danny enters inebriated there.]

| | | |
|---|---|---|
| Surabhi | : | Why are you here? |
| Danny | : | Don't you recognize me? Our Mahatma Gandhi is sitting here. You were delivering lectures that day, "Request the people if you want to get votes." We have won the Election. Won't you congratulate us? |
| Surabhi | : | Having been inebriated, why have you come here late at night? |
| Danny | : | Shut up! You and your dad have motivated the people of these ten villages |

to cast their votes against us. Have we been defeated? Tomorrow, our Party's leader, Paramapriya Patnaik, is forming the Ministry.

Surabhi : Will you step out of the place? Or else I will call the villagers.

Danny : Call them. I am sitting here. I will see who will do what to me here.

[Danny sits there.]

Kulu : (entering)...Danny, let's go.

Danny : She is threatening me in the name of the villagers. You can also sit here.

[Danny helps Kulu sit here.]

Kulu : Tell me, "I am ready to move when you go."

Danny : Kulu, you are a rascal. When we were enjoying liquor, you incited me. Now, you seem to be a gentleman.

Kulu : (Helping Danny get up) Let's go...

[Kulu drags Danny. Danny hurriedly leaves the place.]

Danny : Hold on. We have covered a long distance. Won't we touch the flower?

[Danny touches Surabhi's cheek, but she slaps him.]

Danny : You, bitch! ... Do you know whom you have touched?

Sugreeva : I request you all to leave the place, please.

Danny : Shut up! You, idiot! You will soon see how I am ruining her.

[Danny, pushing Sugreeva, moves toward Surabhi. Kulu gets hold of Danny.]

Kulu : Danny, are you mad? Let's move.

[Kulu leads Danny. Danny roars there.]

Danny : (From outside) I will ruin her on the main road.

[Surabhi cries, hiding her face in humiliation. Sugreeva Babu says helplessly.]

Sugreeva : O My God! What's all this happening here?

[Light off]

## SCENE-X

[It's Surabhi's house. Sugreeva Babu is listening to the news from the transistor (radio). He is waiting for Surabhi's return from school. She has yet to return from school, though it is evening.]

Announcement : (Record) Now Chief Minister Paramapriya Patnaik addresses the people of the State.

[Paramapriya delivers a speech immediately, and he appears to stand from a different zone in the T.V. In a single frame in the T.V., if he had delivered the speech, it could have been more effective. That T. V. may be of a Railway Platform or an Information Centre.]

Paramapriya : Namaskar to all the people of the State. I am grateful to you for all of you have helped the Jana Sevak Party win in most places in the Election as the party president. I have got a chance to serve you all as the Chief Minister of the State. I am determined to execute all my responsibilities smoothly. We have many issues in our State. My priority is to safeguard the public interest against the wild massacre run by the 'S.I.F.O.' extremists. I have already planned for that. With your help, we can remove the 'S.I.F.O.' extremists from the State within one year.

[Surabhi enters, covering her entire body with a shawl. She is gang-raped and ruined. Sugreeva reduces the volume of the transistor. The Chief Minister continues his speech on the T.V. screen, but the sound diminishes.]

Surabhi : You are very late returning from school. I have sent you a person for the evening. Why don't you say anything? (While crying, Surabhi embraces her dad. Then, the shawl gets disrobed from her body. It is seen from her blouse and sari that someone raped her.)
What do I see, my daughter? What has happened to you?
Surabhi : Dad, they are Anadi Babu's people, Danny and Kulu, who ruined me when I returned from school.

[She cries loudly, and then Sugreeva also cries.]
Sugreeva : No, no...Surabhi...no...
[They are crying together. The speech from the T. V. is also heard clearly.]

Paramapriya : The State has secured first position in the country for the rape of girls and women and the murder and suicidal cases of women in dowry. A woman who is a daughter, a mother, a wife, and a sister to people is worshipped like a goddess following our age-old tradition. I have promised and am determined to protect them. If needed, strict rules will be formed and made public for the safety and security of their lives. The Government alone can't do this. We can serve you more and execute our promises if you extend your kind cooperation to us. I want to thank you for your cooperation. Long live!

[Towards the last paragraph of the CM's speech, Surabhi and Sugreeva cry loudly. The mourning voice of the song saddens the situation.]

[In this scene, a transistor is arranged to hear CM Paramapriya's speech. Sugreeva Babu hears this at home while the others listen to it elsewhere. The director will be meticulous in the scene playing the audio clip while Surabhi returns home after being severely injured. While Surabhi's house is lit, the speech is immediately heard in some other place through the T. V.]

## SCENE-XI

[Recapitulation of the past scenes ends here. The train runs. Mangaraj Babu enters the train compartment. Before that, Doctor Satya and Alok will be there.]

| | | |
|---|---|---|
| Mangaraj | : | Sir, excuse me, if I am correct. You are the Founder of Sanatan Seva Institute. Are you Doctor Satya Sanatan? |
| Satya | : | I am Doctor Satya Sanatana, but I can't recognize you. |
| Mangaraj | : | Right. Sir, I am the journalist Adhikarai Mangaraj. (He extends his hands to |

## The Message | 61

|   |   |
|---|---|
| | shake.) Why are you here? The S.I.F.O. extremists have kidnapped and besieged you. I think you are fine now on the train. |
| Satya | : I am returning from them. |
| Mangaraj | : My God! They have released you now. I want to interview you. (Mangaraj Babu brings out a tape recorder from his bag.) How do they treat a social worker of higher order like you? The entire country watches this news. Please start first; I will send the news after editing it.) |
| Satya | : You know, after the formation of the Ministry under the leadership of Paramapriya Patnaik, he tried to control the extremists. The S.I.F.O. group has become vindictive and kidnapped the great leaders and officers and treated them subsequently as the hostages. I was put under Camp Number VIII. What do you mean by the term 'Camp'? |
| Mangaraj | : Many foreign agencies facilitate the S.I.F.O. movement and spend a lot of money on the members. They have camps in different parts of the country. I have heard that many fighters are controlled under the leadership of a commander at every camp to execute extreme works and commit heinous crimes repeatedly. |
| Satya | : I had been taken from their camp to the dense forest. That was an old, dilapidated, black royal palace. |
| Mangaraj | : Well, it was published in the newspapers that a lady extremist has kidnapped you. |

| Satya | : | (Smiling) Yes, you must have heard the name of famous Freedom Fighter Sugreeva Nayak's daughter, Surabhi. Abducting me from the Ashram hospital, she led me to the S.I.F.O. Camp. |

[Along with the train's speed, the noise increases, and the stage lights are off now.]

## SCENE-XII

[The list of past events starts. The entertainment place of extremists... Doctor Satya is sitting in a room. A senior fellow brings food on a tray for him.]

| Nana | : | Hey Babu...It has been three days...You have not had anything except water. Please have this today. |
| Satya | : | I have denied you to serve any food to me. Why have you brought all this? |
| Nana | : | What sort of people are you? One in the other room eagerly waits for food, whereas you don't like to eat anything. |
| Satya | : | Why are you disturbing me? |
| Nana | : | Do you think they will leave you if you don't eat? |
| Satya | : | When death is inevitable, why will I die having food of some nonsense people? I request you to leave this place. |
| Nana | : | All right. I can understand you. I am leaving now; I am telling you frankly that this is Lion's den...he will assault you soon. He is coming from this side...it will be good if you have food now. |

| | | |
|---|---|---|
| | | [Arun comes. He has a rough-tough body, and his tone has changed.] |
| Arun | : | What's up? Doctor Sahib has started fasting. |
| Nana | : | Yes, Sir, he has not touched anything except water for the last three days. |
| Arun | : | If you don't eat, you know your condition well. Doctor, nobody will be here to mourn you, even if you die shriveled. |
| Satya | : | I know this. |
| | | [Arun gets annoyed with the Doctor's response, but he tries to control it.] |
| Arun | : | If you know this, why are you fasting? |
| Satya | : | 'Fasting' is beyond my comprehension. I don't want to eat; I won't eat. |
| Arun | : | You don't have the desire to live. |
| Satya | : | To eat food only to live is not my habit. |
| Arun | : | (Out of anger roaring) Rascal, you are teaching me moral lessons. You are not eating to live. You are a doctor. It would help if you had the habit of drinking blood from people experiencing poverty. You won't like all this. Is the fat deposited on your body, not the money of the poor and distressed people? Could you respond to me (taking a break)? I know well that sanguinary mosquitoes like you don't have any answer to this. |
| Satya | : | It is better to think of the lunatic's treatment instead of answering their questions. |
| Arun | : | Rascal, are you delivering dialogues? |
| Satya | : | Wah! If I don't speak, you tell me I am |

|       |   |                                                                 |
|-------|---|-----------------------------------------------------------------|
|       |   | not answering. If I answer, you say I am delivering dialogue.   |
| Arun  | : | Are we all mad?                                                 |
| Satya | : | Can one prove the madness of a lunatic through arguments?       |
| Arun  | : | Bastard, you must prove this.                                   |
| Satya | : | If I prove this, do you have the patience to confess?           |
| Arun  | : | Still, you must prove this here.                                |
| Satya | : | All these don't have any value or meaning for the people who have lost their mental balance. |
| Arun  | : | Shut up!                                                        |
| Satya | : | Yes, I prefer silence to talking. You can kill me if you want. Otherwise, please leave me alone. |
| Arun  | : | (Bringing out a pistol out of anger) Can you see this? Can Fighter Arun trigger this pistol at any time? I will use this once the S.I.F.O. Chief orders me. Nana, you listen to me…you go placing the food before him. I will take it seriously if he doesn't take food by tomorrow.<br>[Arun leaves.] |
| Nana  | : | Hey Babu, have you seen his Lion's form? You work as per his orders if you want something good to happen. Otherwise, you will see how the Lion hunts its prey. |

[Nana serves the food on a plate before the doctor and a small kid enters there. He masked his face. He has a toy gun in his hands. That kid shows that gun at Nana's back.]

| | | |
|---|---|---|
| Alok | : | (At Nana's ears) Fire… (Nana gets annoyed.) …I am afraid of this child. |
| Nana | : | What is happening here? |
| Alok | : | Shut up! We feel disturbed. It was a poor man's attack. (Showing the gun) |
| Nana | : | I don't like any 'attack'. Why are you showing that towards me? Take that away from my front. |
| Alok | : | Coward! You die many times before death comes to you. I can't insult my sten gun killing you. |
| Nana | : | What do you think of me? Am I at your disposal? |
| Nana | : | Nana, who is this child? |
| Nana | : | Nobody knows, Sir? I am still trying to figure out his parents. They have kidnapped him from somewhere. |
| Satya | : | Have they kidnapped him? |
| Nana | : | Sir, some children like him are in every camp. They dispatch secret letters, but I am afraid of this child. |
| Satya | : | Why? |
| Nana | : | Sometimes, he is being handed over the real gun. He kills the hens alive. These people kill people like insects. He will also do the same once he grows up. |
| Satya | : | With whom does he stay here? |
| Nana | : | With Lion and Surabhi madam. They encouraged him to do so. This boy may kill anybody at any time. I am always afraid of him. I leave now. You can have your food. |

[When Nana leaves, this boy stands in his front with a gun.]
But, if you threaten me like this, I will tell the commander.
[Nana leaves; the boy laughs at his fear.]

| | | |
|---|---|---|
| Satya | : | (To the boy) Please come. |
| Alok | : | No |
| Satya | : | Won't you come to me? |
| Alok | : | You have been hungry for the last three days. You will rebuke me. |
| Satya | : | Why will I scold you when I am angry? |
| Alok | : | Lion scolds me in hunger. Surabhi Madam says that when one returns from work or is hungry, and if you reach them, they will rebuke you. |
| Satya | : | Oh, for that only you won't come. |
| Alok | : | I have told you once that a hungry man is an angry man. |
| Satya | : | I am fasting. Am I angry? |
| Alok | : | No, your anger may be in your mind. I won't go. (Running) |
| Satya | : | Well, listen to me. If I break my fasting, will you come to me? |
| Alok | : | Yes, you have your food first, and then, I will come to you. |
| Satya | : | (Taking a glass of water and eating) Is it OK? |
| Alok | : | (Nodding his head) No…no…you have not taken anything. You must eat more. You must finish all this. |
| Satya | : | I have been fasting for so long; I will fall sick if I take all this at once. You will see that I am gradually taking food from today onwards. Come…come to me. |

| | | |
|---|---|---|
| Alok | : | (Coming closer to him) What? |
| Satya | : | What's your name? |
| Alok | : | My name is…Ammunition…explosion… |
| Satya | : | Is it a name? |
| Alok | : | Can I tell my father's name? |
| Satya | : | Do you know your father's name? |
| Alok | : | My father's name is Government. |
| Satya | : | Government? |
| Alok | : | Yes |
| Satya | : | What's your mother's name? |
| Alok | : | My mother's name is Democracy. |
| Satya | : | Your father's name is 'Government', and your mother's is 'Democracy'!! Who has taught you all this? |
| Alok | : | Can I tell you, my address? At…post… Independent India. |
| Satya | : | These names don't sound good. These are different from the proper names. |
| Alok | : | Lion, Commander and Bul have given my names. Do you know 'Why'? |
| Satya | : | Why? |
| Alok | : | Some people unitedly assaulted a girl. The police arrested them. The case was sub judice. The final verdict was made public after a long time. There was no positive result. They were released from the court without any punishment. I was born after that. |
| Satya | : | That's why you are named 'Explosion'. |
| Alok | : | Why not…nothing was finalized in the court. That girl died after giving birth to me. Then, I became the child of the Government. |

| | | |
|---|---|---|
| Satya | : | All right…leave it…they have taught you all this. Have you learnt anything else? |
| Alok | : | *Dhos…dhos…dhos*…fighting… [I know how to trigger a sten gun and get involved in wrestling.] |
| Satya | : | These activities are not good. |
| Alok | : | You don't know anything. Three giants stay on the other side of the forest. They will harm me if I don't know how to use the bombs and rifles. |
| Satya | : | I have also come from the other side of the forest. I have not seen them anywhere. |
| Alok | : | Haven't you seen them yet? One giant of them is a politician, one a capitalist, and one a government servant. Haven't you seen them? They have their grown-up children, bank balances, and soldiers. They have one persona at their home… one before the society. They are fond of drinking the poor's blood. |
| Arun | : | (Entering) Hey…what are you doing here? Who has opened the door? [Nana enters hearing Arun's voice.] Where have you gone, when the door is open, Rascal? Are you under the spell of ganja in the morning? Where were you opening the door? [Arun steps out, dragging the child.] |
| Nana | : | Yes, because of you, I have been rebuked. Let me leave now, closing the door. If you want to have, you can; otherwise not. [Nana leaves.] Light off |

# SCENE-XIII

[Here is a room of the extremists' camp. Anadisundar's eyes, hands, and legs are fastened. Bul drags him and puts him in that Cell. Anadisundar falls.]

| | | |
|---|---|---|
| Anadi | : | It hurts me a lot. Where are you taking me blindfolded and with my limbs tied? |
| Bul | : | Don't shout. (Bul clears the pistol.) |
| Anadi | : | Sir!!! |
| Bul | : | Shut up! Sit down here. |
| Anadi | : | Yes, I am sitting. Please release me from these shackles. I have suffered a lot. |
| Bul | : | No, not now, but at the time of taking your food- |
| Anadi | : | Sir, I request you…please open this blindfold from my eyes or else I will be blind. |

[He tries to get hold of his legs while groping.]

| | | |
|---|---|---|
| Bul | : | (Throwing him) Bastard, you are talking nonsense. Shut up. |
| Anadi | : | (Crying) I refused to be the minister. Our Sir didn't listen to me. He made me the minister forcefully. Please release me now; I will resign from the post.<br>[After sometimes after silence] Whether it's day or night, sir? |
| Bul | : | What does it matter? |
| Anadi | | How can I know, I am blindfolded? I am hirsty now. Please give me a glass of water. |
| Bul | : | Now you will take your food…you will also drink water. |

| | | |
|---|---|---|
| Anadi | : | Sir, won't you release us? I joined politics without knowing anything. I am an unlettered fellow. (After a while) Sir, what's your name please? Aren't you from our State? |
| Bul | : | Why are you so talkative now? |
| Anadi | : | (Taking a breath) What's the time now? |
| Bul | : | (Giving a blow in irritation) Do you have any respect for time or not? |
| Anadi | : | Yes, I understand. You have got a blow. Don't ask me before one O'clock. Otherwise, I would be flogged. |
| Bul | : | Again, talking nonsense? |
| Anadi | : | Pardon me, Sir. Though I try not to say anything, I can't do so.<br>[Nana brings food on a tray.] |
| Bul | : | You hear, you will close his mouth with a cloth after eating food. He is always talking nonsense.<br>[Bul leaves.] |
| Anadi | : | Yes, Sir…do that. I can't be so talkative. |
| Nana | : | (Opening his mouth and hands) Please come, Minister Sahib. Have the food quickly. |
| Anadi | : | Oh, Sir! May God bless you! |
| Nana | : | Oh, Sir, nobody is here. If Jagannatha comes here, he will also experience the same situation. |
| Anadi | : | You must be a Brahmin, Sir. |
| Nana | : | Forget that…I am cooking for the slaughterers and washing the utensils. Tell me, I am a Dalit. I am Dalit. |

[Anadi eats food. Taking a break from food…]

| | | |
|---|---|---|
| Anadi | : | Sir, you are from our State. (Requesting him) Please release me after having a word with them. Be kind and compassionate towards me. |
| Nana | : | *The name of Hari in Lankapuri.* (A prostitute preaching) Have your food fast…I must take care of others. |
| Anadi | : | (Holding his legs) Please release me at any cost. I will hand over to you what I hoarded through extortion or bribery. |
| Nana | : | Have you seen the mouse trap? It is of iron…if anybody enters there, he will come out a lash. Day by day, one becomes prey. |
| Anadi | : | Do you work here, Sir? |
| Nana | : | Having won the Election, you have become a Minister. Why are you using the word 'Sir' repeatedly to me? Again, you are asking me whether I have joined the job here. Can anyone do the job in the *Yamalaya*? |

[Commander and Lion start laughing together at a distance. The sound of cockfighting is also heard.]

> Hello… you can take your food fast. They are watching the cockfighting. Once I am called from that side, everything will be over.
> [Nana leaves the spot.]
> Light off

## SCENE-XIV

Commander : (Pointing at a place on the map) Look at the spot on the seashore. Near that spot is a dilapidated building. They will unload the ammunition packets there one day before the scheduled date. Your responsibility is to bring all those to our headquarters via that building.

Surabhi : Yes, Commander. I can load the ammunition in the truck and bring it to our headquarters, but I need at least eight to ten fighters for this operation.

Commander : You will be provided. Bul will also be with you. But be careful of the instructions of the S.I.F.O. Chief that the police patrolling on the sea beach are regular and strict.

Surabhi : Last time, Police Patrolling was also very strict. Commander, we were still successful. I am fully confident that if the Fighters are with the rifles, they can obstruct hundreds of police personnel.

Commander : Yes, each Fighter should be with this type of confidence. The S.I.F.O. Chief is pleased with the fighters dedicated to serving the country like you. Plan your strategy with Bul. Lion and I will monitor the entire operation process.

Bul : We will be successful, Commander! Don't worry about it.

[Surabhi and Bul leave the spot. Commander talks to somebody wirelessly on one of the room's corners.]

| | | |
|---|---|---|
| Commander | : | Hello…0091…hello…hello…I am speaking from Camp number VIII…hello…hello…Headquarters. |
| | | [Arun comes to stand near Commander.] |
| Commander | : | What happened, Lion? Do you have any information about Suresh? |
| Arun | : | Yes, I have, but unfortunate news. |
| Commander | : | What's that? |
| Arun | : | The day before last night, the police force red-handed him. |
| Commander | : | Are you sure? |
| Arun | : | Yes, I am. The Police have taken Fighter Mishra and Suresh from Camp No. VI. But I need to figure out their whereabouts. |
| Commander | : | Lion, Suresh needs to be stronger. Now, I am afraid he may speak the truth if beaten hard. Oh…I am worried…What can I do? |
| Arun | : | Lion, you think of Suresh as weak. Though he has a weakness for wine, he will never be disloyal to the S.I.F.O. |
| Commander | : | Well, what do you think of doing for him? |
| Arun | : | We must know Suresh's whereabouts from our informer at the Police Department. For that, we must pay him a lot. After that, I can carry off him from the Police Station strategically. |
| Commander | : | Alright! I am contacting the Police Station. Then we will plan accordingly. |

[The sound of the wireless is heard. Commander holds the receiver.]

| | | |
|---|---|---|
| Commander | : | Hello...Camp Commander No. 08 speaking...hello...(Over to headquarters) |

[In one's voice, a metallic sound is heard from the opposite direction.]

| | | |
|---|---|---|
| Wireless | : | Note down that No. 1 Suresh Singh is killed in the Police Custody. The Police killed him while beating. Suresh Singh, Fighter No. 13002, is dead, informed by headquarters...Over. |
| Commander | : | (Shouting) No...no...no |
| Arun | : | Commander, this can't be true. Police can't kill him like this. |
| Commander | : | Yes, Lion. This is the message from headquarters. Your patriotic friend is martyred today. The Government's servant police have killed him. |
| Arun | : | The government must pay massive compensation for Suresh's life. We have taken it seriously and will answer them firmly. |
| Commander | : | Yes. I will decide after having a word with the S.I.F.O. Chief. Those who are in jail will be killed one by one, and their dead bodies will be thrown on the principal avenues of the Capital. |

[Commander will be ruder and more ferocious while using this dialogue.]

| | | |
|---|---|---|
| Arun | : | Yes, Commander; "Once S.I.F.O. is vindictive and revengeful, what the consequence can be." Let the Government know this. |

[All the lights are focused on Commander and Arun.]

Light off

# SCENE-XV

[This is the Cell where Anadi resides. His hands are not tied, and his eyes are not blindfolded. Arun drags Doctor Satya to the Cell.]

| | | |
|---|---|---|
| Arun | : | Doctor Satya Sanatana! Do you know why you have been brought to this spot? |
| Satya | : | To a hostage whether to know or not all this is meaningless. |
| Arun | : | Our Commander tells us that you are a writer. You have written a lot on social reformation. Today, you will write a letter to the government on our behalf—the gentleman whose face lying downward before you will take this to the Government. |
| Anadi | : | Yes, please release me soon. I will hand over this to the Chief Minister directly. |
| Satya | : | I must write that the S.I.F.O. Fighters are using the hostages in their favour. |
| Arun | : | No. You will write what I will dictate to you. You are the Chief Minister's friend. Thus, your handwritten letter will never go in vain. |
| Satya | : | No, I can't write all those. |
| Arun | : | (Shouting suddenly out of anger) Wait for a while, Doctor! You will see what Fighter Arun can do ... whether you can or not. |
| Anadi | : | You can say 'yes' to write, Doctor Babu. After I hand over the letter to the Chief Minister, I will convince him to release |

|         | all the Fighters. You will also be released from there. |
|---------|---|

[Arun suddenly slaps Anadi.]

Arun : You, shut up! Your government servants, Police have killed our fighters beating and flogging in the jail. The Chief Minister has betrayed the S.I.F.O. group for not releasing our fighters unconditionally. Today, this Doctor will write down the letter, and your dead body will be sent to the Government with this letter.

[Arun points the pistol at Anadi.]

Anadi : No, don't kill me, Sir. Could you not show me that? Please pardon me this time, Sir. No...no...

[Anadi can't cry out of fear; his voice is choked. After that, there is the sound of fire and Anadisundar's cry. Then silence pervades.]

Arun : Doctor, please pick up this pen and paper. Pick up that pen. I can't bear so much arrogance. (Shouting) pick up. Otherwise, I will break down your limbs.

[Arun beats Doctor. Alok looks at all this, hiding himself in a place.]

Rascal! won't you listen to me after being flogged so much?

[Again beating]

So much arrogance...so much pride...

[Doctor loses his sense because of flagellation.]

But now, he is senseless. Dragging him, you shut in that room.

[Arun leaves. Alok stands closer to the doctor. Looking at his situation, he starts crying. He tries to break down the toy gun in his hands. Bul takes Doctor dragging to that room. Alok looks at the path where Bul is marching ahead.]

## SCENE-XVI

[It's night. On the sea beach, Police Officer Gautam and Constable Priyanath come from two opposite directions of the stage, searching for someone else.]

Gautam : (In choked voice) What happened?
Priyanath : I can't see anybody here. The Police force have besieged this area. They must disguise/ camouflage themselves somewhere nearby.
Gautam : All right. Go to that side. I am going on this side. There is a hilltop near our jeep. There is a searchlight. Once I hint at you, you will switch on the light. OK.

[Both move in different directions. After some time, Surabhi and Bul enter stealthily or surreptitiously. They whisper and hide themselves, seeing the police. Then, Gautam returns, having searched the surroundings. Surabhi talks wirelessly. Bul watches the Police's movement.]

Surabhi : (Holding the wireless set) Hello... Commander...the truck is loaded with our ammunition packets, but we can't leave the place. Police Jeep patrols here. Of course, they have not seen our vehicle. Over...
Commander : (From the other side) Alright. Stop there.

Watch the Police's movement. Arun and I, observing the Police's position, are reaching there soon. Wait until we reach there. Over…

[Bul walks.]

Bul : Quick, Surabhi. Police Jeep comes to this side…be careful.

[One side of the stage is lit with the light of the jeep. Surabhi and Bul try to run. There is a siren. Surabhi falls at the police firing. She still runs…the stage echoes in the Jeep's siren.]

## SCENE-XVII

[On the cyclorama at the backside of the stage, Surabhi groans in pain, sleeping on a cot. Arun and Alok are there. Then, there is the sound of a motorbike. Commander and Arun enter from opposite directions. They start talking before the cyclorama.]

Arun : Has Doctor Rao come?

Commander : No, Lion, it's our bad luck. Doctor Rao is not at home. He has gone to Camp Number-V for someone's treatment.

Arun : Oh My God! That means he is 300 kilometers away from here. There is no possibility of his return tonight.

Commander : I have brought all the instruments needed for the operation from his Nursing Home. Bul has taken my bike to find him.

Arun : A bullet is shot at Surabhi's abdomen. Bleeding doesn't stop from there, though we tried our best.

[Surabhi's groaning is heard. Arun and Commander went inside and returned from there.]

Commander : Surabhi will be right tomorrow, though she groans in pain. I think no mishap will happen to her.

Arun : Surabhi's condition does not seem reasonable to me. Please allow me to find a doctor in the city.

Commander : No…no Arun. We must take decisions carefully with our adversaries. Don't be emotional. It won't be a wise decision to go to the town and to find a doctor for an operation on this night.

Arun : But there is no certainty about our S.I.F.O.'s Doctor Rao's reach here, Commander.

Commander : Why don't you understand, Arun? Surabhi is injured at the Police firing. Had the Police Jeep not been punctured, none of them could have returned alive. Now, throughout the city, the Police must be vigilant in every Nursing Home and Hospital. If you go to the city at this stage, you will be easily nabbed by the Police.

Arun : No…Commander, we must save her life by some other means. I have brought Surabhi to this 'S.I.F.O.'. I can't tolerate her breathing last before me like this. We must do something.
[The door is knocked on.]

Commander : Who's knocking on the door so hard?

Nana : That Babu in that room tells me to open the door.

| | | |
|---|---|---|
| Commander | : | Why is he telling you to open the door? |
| Nana | : | He wants to see Surabhi Madam, Sir. |
| Arun | : | Yes, I still need you. He is a doctor. We can request him for help. |
| Commander | : | But why will he help us? We have kidnapped him from his home; especially Surabhi herself has done this work. |
| Arun | : | No, Commander. Please don't deny it. (To Nana) you go and bring him from his room. |
| Nana | : | Sir (He leaves.) |
| Commander | : | Arun, you see. You are calling the Doctor but be careful…he may be dangerous to Surabhi. He may kill her in the name of treatment. We should wait for our doctor Rao to return. |
| Satya | : | (Entering) Where is the patient? |
| Commander | : | The patient is in that room…how can you help us? |
| Satya | : | Let me see the patient. Please don't waste time asking me what I can do or not. |
| Arun | : | Please come, Come with me.<br>[Doctor enters the room after Arun and returns.] |
| Satya | : | (Having seen the patient) The patient is serious. |
| Commander | : | (Out of irritation) How do you know? |
| Satya | : | If we don't do the operation immediately, there is less possibility of her life. |
| Commander | : | How can you be so confident that she will die soon if we don't do her operation now? |
| Satya | : | Are you using a knife or a pair of scissors? |

|            |   | She will be anaesthetized before her operation starts. |
|------------|---|---|
| Arun       | : | All instruments are with us in our vehicle. |
| Satya      | : | Bring all those without wasting time. |
| Commander  | : | But who will do the operation? |
| Satya      | : | Yes, I will. Do what I say without wasting any time. Every moment is precious now. |
| Commander  | : | Arun…This Doctor will do the operation. Who will guarantee that the operation will be successful? |
| Satya      | : | As a Doctor, I will try my best to be successful in the operation, but I am not the God who will guarantee you. |
| Commander  | : | I know nothing will happen to Surabhi till tomorrow, but if you want to blackmail us, … |
| Arun       | : | You know well what the consequence of that will be. So, Doctor, be careful… |
| Satya      | : | (Shouting) You cowards…who are you threatening to? Being afraid of death, you hide yourselves in darkness. Why do you think that the entire world will be frightened of death? Death…My foot. You have the lust for your own life…You are forgetting your responsibility for one of your friends who is struggling with death. You are thinking of your safety and security. I hate you, mad fellows. Doctor Satya Sanatan hates beasts like you who have no humanitarian values. Let your patient breathe her last. Let her go to hell. I can't help you. [Doctor leaves.] |

Arun : Commander, please allow him to do her operation. Please request him.

[Arun moves in the direction Doctor returns.]

## SCENE-XVIII

[The entire scene will be on the cyclorama at the back of the stage. The shadows of the actors will be visible. At the beginning of the stage, Surabhi is found sleeping on a cot. Doctor Satya Sanatan is doing an operation. Surabhi's pain is heard. Arun holds Surabhi tightly at the time of operation. Alok is standing nearby. After the operation is over, the Doctor ties the bandage. Suddenly, Surabhi gets up and cries in pain and then sleeps on the cot as earlier. There is pin-drop silence. Only Arun's voice is heard, 'Surabhi, Surabhi'. Commander, Bul and others run from the other room and surround Surabhi's bed.]

## SCENE-XIX

[Doctor Satya Sanatan is busy writing with a piece of paper. Alok stands before him with a rose in his hand.]

Satya : Come...won't you come to me...I have seen something good today. In your hand is a rose instead of a gun.
Alok : Madam has given.
Satya : Wah, it's nice.
Alok : Can you say who I brought this flower for?
Satya : For whom? For your friend, Lion

| | | |
|---|---|---|
| Alok | : | No, I have brought it for you. You have saved our Madam's life. |
| Satya | : | Alright…this is a gift for me. I want to give you something. |
| Alok | : | No…no…I won't receive anything from you. If Lion knows, he will scold me. |
| Satya | : | I will give you something that nobody other than you can know. |
| Alok | : | Can Commander not know? |
| Satya | : | No |
| Alok | : | (Looking outside) Nobody is here. Give me what you want. |
| Satya | : | I will give you a new name. It is 'Alok'. |
| Alok | : | Can you repeat the name? |
| Satya | : | 'Alok'…If I call you 'Alok, can you come or not? |
| Alok | : | Yes…I will…What are you writing? |
| Satya | : | Poem' I am writing a letter in your name. |
| Alok | : | Do you know 'poem'? |
| Satya | : | Yes |
| Alok | : | Can you help me learn? |
| Satya | : | After writing this song, I will teach you. |
| Alok | : | Can you say what you have written in my name? |
| Satya | : | I have written one stanza…will you hear? |
| Alok | : | Yes |
| Satya | : | (Reciting)<br>"Have all sorts of arrangements for Alok today, for he has lost his path in darkness, Accompany him getting hold of his hands, for he is wandering aimlessly." |
| Alok | : | I will tell Madam that you are writing poems for me. |

| | | |
|---|---|---|
| Satya | : | What is Madam doing? |
| Alok | : | She was telling me to come to you…I will call her. |
| Satya | : | No…no…I have denied her to get up from bed. I will go to her at the right time. |
| Alok | : | (Holding the paper on which the poem was written) I am taking this. I will show it to Madam. |

[Alok leaves.]

| | | |
|---|---|---|
| Satya | : | Hey…Alok…Alok…that is of one stanza only. |

[Again, Satya Sanatan starts writing the poem on another paper. From the background, the song is heard.]

| | | |
|---|---|---|
| Song | : | "Have all sorts of arrangements for Alok today, for he has lost his path in darkness, Accompany him getting hold of his hands, for he is wandering aimlessly. Having seen some tears on life's path, He has forgotten how to smile. Having seen thorns in the rose garden, He had forgotten its smell. Show him the way to sip nectar, He is internally burning. Have all sorts of arrangements for Alok…" |

[Surabhi stands near the door. Satya is busy writing the poem. He sees Surabhi suddenly.]

| | | |
|---|---|---|
| Satya | : | O Surabhi, why have you come to me leaving your bed? |

| | | |
|---|---|---|
| Surabhi | : | I am indeed well now. You have compelled me to lie in bed. |
| Satya | : | After the operation, the soar is dried, but you will rest for some days. |
| Surabhi | : | I have many incomplete projects that need to be completed. |
| Satya | : | When you are my patient, you must keep up my words. |
| Surabhi | : | That's why I am still lying in bed. Otherwise, I would have gone outside last week. |
| Satya | : | I know that you are interested in stepping out. |
| Surabhi | : | Do you know? |
| Satya | : | Yes, kidnapping and murdering… |
| Surabhi | : | We are all S.I.F.O.'s Fighters. Anybody can talk about us. |
| Satya | : | No…I can tell you what you have decided to execute now. |
| Surabhi | : | Perhaps Lion (Arun) has told you everything. |
| Satya | : | I have not been allowed to interact with anybody except you. Then, every S.I.F.O. Fighter, especially Commander and Arun, hates talking to me. |
| Surabhi | : | No. Meanwhile, Arun respects you very much. |
| Satya | : | Maybe…I have been very compassionate to him, for he has come down to the level of an animal from the level of human beings. I feel pity for him. |
| Surabhi | : | It is natural for those who don't know about our lives to think. Leave it…you |

| | | |
|---|---|---|
| | | are telling me you can say what I have planned to do…please say. |
| Satya | : | You want to take revenge on someone now? |
| Surabhi | : | Who can you say? |
| Satya | : | (Smiling) What does it matter if your decision is not changed based on what I say? |
| Surabhi | : | No…you can't say anything. |
| Satya | : | (Emphatically) Yes, I can. |
| Surabhi | : | But how? |
| Satya | : | Every human being has one more eye other than these two. That's the 'Third Eye'. You don't know how to use them… but I have known this. Thus, I can tell you what you are going to do. |
| Surabhi | : | Please say… |
| Satya | : | You are excited to kill that Police Officer who fired at you when you were transporting the ammunition and explosives. |
| Surabhi | : | Yes…but how did you know? I have not discussed this with anybody except Lion. |
| Satya | : | I have the 'Third Eye'. |
| Surabhi | : | Can you say whether I can kill him or not? |
| Saya | : | Yes, I can say. You can't. |
| Surabhi | : | No…you want to brainwash me. |
| Satya | : | I am only activating your brain's subtle parts (cords). |
| Surabhi | : | But I am determined in my work and will be till my target is achieved. |
| Satya | : | No one can be determined in anger and pain. |

| | | |
|---|---|---|
| Surabhi | : | I am consecrated in S.I.F.O.'s Ideology of Revolution. I will be working for a new world. |
| Satya | : | But I am only the votary or devotee of one great eternal culture; I will always search for the light for the immortal world. |
| Surabhi | : | (Shouting) no…no…(Crying) I can't forgive him. He has ruined me. |
| Satya | : | Still, you must forgive him. |
| Surabhi | : | You have never bled in the pains of injustice. You have never seen the plight of the lower-middle-class people like us. You can never understand how much we are insulted and neglected daily. Still, we struggle to live. |
| Satya | : | I know. I can understand everything. Still, you must change your decision. |
| Surabhi | : | No…you must listen to the injustices that happened to me individually. Then, I can change my decision as you will say. |
| Satya | : | How will I benefit from hearing all the past incidents? I am still ready to listen to your anguishes and agonies, hoping to relax you for a while. |
| Surabhi | : | I am the daughter of the renowned freedom fighter Sugreeva Nayak. Though we had everything, for our father's ideology and attitude to serve the people, I spent my childhood life and college life in Baudapur village. In the last election campaign, our Minister of Culture, Anadisundar, asked my father to request a vote. When some of his associates, |

|  |  |
|---|---|
|  | antisocial youngsters, entering our home insulted us, we strongly opposed them. For that only when I returned from the school in one evening, … |
| Satya | : That story…I have read from the newspapers. I have also heard they were arrested after a strong and healthy discourse in the state assembly. |
| Surabhi | : The Opposition Party's shouting… the arrest to befool the public does not make sense, Doctor Sahib. They were the minister's people. Doctors and Police together framed reports so that they all got released. I became pregnant by their wild lust. At that stage, my father hoped they would be punished in the Honourable High Court. But that didn't happen. Instead, they all got bail from the court and proudly walked before us. My father could not take food out of shame and insult. At last, he died. Before he died, he was repeatedly saying one point like a lunatic.<br>[In Sugreeva's tone from the background echoed that message.] |
| Sugreeva | : (Voice) What is the principal duty of a King or an administrator, my daughter? It is to safeguard the properties and lives of ordinary people. But in this country, they are far away from this… the administrators are here instrumental in spreading terror, menace, threat, etc. They plunder people's properties and |

| | | |
|---|---|---|
| | | lives. It's better to do suicide than living in this country. |
| Surabhi | : | My father died with this kind of incoherent talk. After that, I joined S.I.F.O. with Arun. |
| Satya | : | Being a S.I.F.O. Fighter, you want to take revenge. Is it so? |
| Surabhi | : | No, Doctor, I have not got any mental peace. The Police Officer who framed the report, after inquiring, still lives. It is more surprising that the Police Officer fired me on that day. I can't sit silently unless I give him a lesson. No, never. [Surabhi's eyes glaze like a fierce tiger.] |
| Satya | : | But, if you kill that Police Officer… Danny…Kulu, will your problem be solved? |
| Surabhi | : | It may not be, but these can't be extended for so long. The S.I.F.O. will confront this. The way they are torturing the innocent people of the country, we are determined to fight against them. |
| Satya | : | It is good that you will confront them as a group. But you are spreading terrorism in the country in the name of facing them… you are denying the hopes of this eternal world in the search for the new world. |
| Surabhi | : | No, Doctor, I am indebted to you for my operation…I am ready to donate what you want for that. But please don't weaken me by listening to your traditional moral lessons. I can't hear all this right now. |

| | | |
|---|---|---|
| | | [Surabhi leaves the place hurriedly.] |
| Satya | : | Who is standing there? |
| Arun | : | I am Arun. |
| | | [Arun enters with a newspaper.] |
| Satya | : | Were you listening to our discourse hiding there? |
| Arun | : | I came here to give you a newspaper. I stood there in the darkness to listen to the arguments and counterarguments made by you and Surabhi, respectively. |
| Satya | : | What's the news? Your Chief has sent you a message to fire at me. |
| Arun | : | No…I want to release you from here. |
| Satya | : | Has the S.I.F.O.'s Chief decided to release me? |
| Arun | : | They have yet to decide, but I can help them understand. |
| Satya | : | But I won't go like that. |
| Arun | : | No need to be afraid of. You will safely reach your home. |
| Satya | : | If I leave the place, I must accompany you all. |
| Arun | : | What do you mean? |
| Satya | : | You all must surrender before the Police. |
| Arun | : | Doctor, you see…You have saved Surabhi's life. That is true. That does not mean we will betray S.I.F.O. and go by your words. |
| Arun | : | Please see, you may not get a chance like this. Be ready to leave the spot. |
| Satya | : | No, I can't go like a thief. |
| Arun | : | You see here…It would help if you went to your home. Your only beloved |

| | | |
|---|---|---|
| | | daughter is on her deathbed. She is earnestly searching for you. Her photo, at her request, has been published in the newspaper. |
| Satya | : | This is false...I can't believe that my daughter will write a letter like this. |
| Arun | : | She has written, (Reading the letter) "Hello Brothers, those who have kidnapped my father...as your small sister, I request you all, please..." |
| Satya | : | Stop it. I have never taught my daughter to request others for her father's life. The press or police personnel may force her to write like this. |
| Arun | : | I request you now...Currently, you don't give us empty morals. Please be ready to go. |
| Satya | : | I have told you once...I can't leave the place secretly. |
| Arun | : | But why? Why are you so obstinate? |
| Satya | : | It's not my obstinacy but my duty. I have the same responsibility towards society as I have for my family. |
| Arun | : | Oh, morals, morals, morals!!! Surabhi has heard this for an hour. Again, you have started before me. What right do you have to help us listen to you? |
| Satya | : | As a doctor, I am responsible for treating patients, so I have the right to instruct society as a writer. |
| Arun | : | But why are you so obstinate/ arrogant, Doctor? Why do you think that you are only intelligent? Will the theory you |

| | | |
|---|---|---|
| | | have developed or proposed hold good forever? |
| Satya | : | This is because I am fully confident in my theory. I have compared that with other theories. |
| Arun | : | I can't tolerate you anymore. Doctor…I can't tolerate your self-conceit. |
| Satya | : | I know you can't because you commit crimes and are being governed by your extreme swindling. |
| Arun | : | Crime? What kind of crimes do we commit? Doctor…explain to us individually; otherwise, squeezing your neck, I will stop your voice forever.<br>[Arun squeezes Doctor's neck. The Doctor releases himself from Arun.] |
| Satya | : | I will alert you to the crimes you have committed individually. You don't dare to accept your crimes/faults because your education has blinded you. |
| Arun | : | I ask you, "What are my faults?" |
| Satya | : | You think murdering others is a courageous act. You want to prove that you are above the law and the Government. You believe that taking revenge for an insult is heroic deed. But you are afraid of society. You have lost your courage to face the reality of life. Your future has terrified you so much that you are ready to ruin or make bloodstain your present. |
| Arun | : | Doctor, keeping in view the future, making the present bloodstain is the other name of revenge/ revolution. |

| | | |
|---|---|---|
| Satya | : | No…selling yourself after some weak doctrines stolen from the foreign land and shouting 'Revolution, Revolution', revolution won't take place. |
| Arun | : | What is 'Revolution'? Do you know what it is? |
| Satya | : | It's the transformation from evil to good and from the path of degeneration to righteousness. It is the cultural reformation from nasty to beautiful and eternal. Arun, revolution is not the slogan of change overnight like a storm. We can't attain revolution in a day. Mental preparedness and perseverance are needed. After all, people's support is needed for revolution. |
| Arun | : | We have been fighting to release innocent people from their exploitation. Why do you think that the public won't support us? |
| Satya | : | Nobody can reach the public with guns. Public opinion is like an infant. To win their hearts, one must practise love and compassion, give up pride and serve them. Arun, the truth one must remember is that violence is created from violence, love from love, and light from light always leads to light. |
| Arun | : | That means what one lakh Fighters of S.I.F.O. have done so far is all wrong. |
| Satya | : | It's not what they have been doing, but what you are doing needs corrections. Staying in a foreign land, they fulfil their |

wishes and keep aside your objectives. Have you ever seen your 'Chief'? Have you ever enquired about the place where food, ammunition, and weapons are prepared? Nay...have you ever been given a chance to explore this? Why are they so sympathetic to this country?

Arun : No...Doctor...no. I am getting tired of hearing all this. There is no need to know everything in an extremist's life. They can remember only the injustice that happened to them. He will declare that he works hard to free the land or society from exploitation. I won't listen to your words...we have been martyred before fighting. For the martyrs, there is no value in a new life. We must remember only... we are terrorists...we are extremists...we are the frightful fire sparks or revolting firebrands.

[Arun gets disturbed. Doctor's dialogue gets echoed in Arun's ear..." For your food, weapons... Arun leaves hurriedly. A streak of smile shines in Doctor's face."]

Light off

## SCENE-XX

[Here is the Commander's room in the extremists' camp. Commander and Bul are talking to each other.]

| | | |
|---|---|---|
| Bul | : | What decision have you taken about Doctor Sahib? It won't be good for S.I.F.O. to keep him here for many days. |
| Commander | : | Yes, Bul, I have understood that. If he stays here many days, his influence over our Fighters will be strong. But without our Chief's permission, we can neither kill nor release him. |
| Bul | : | You can talk to our Chief regarding him and confirm us quickly. |
| Commander | : | Alright. Our Chief is now abroad. I will contact him and finalize this. Be careful about their movements. Okay. |

[Symbolic sounds are heard on the wireless. Commander starts talking holding the receiver.]

Hello...hello...This is number eight....

Light off

## SCENE-XXI

[Here's the same room of the Extremist's camp. It's midnight. The Doctor is sleeping...Surabhi comes.]

| | | |
|---|---|---|
| Surabhi | : | (In choked voice) Doctor Sahib...Doctor Sahib...Get up, Doctor Sahib... |
| Satya | : | Surabhi...why are you here at midnight? What has happened to you? |

| | | |
|---|---|---|
| Surabhi | : | I came here late at night to pass you an important message. Commander has instructed to kill you tomorrow. |
| Satya | : | Oh, that's why you earnestly want me to be released from this camp. |
| Surabhi | : | No, you have been so careless about 'death' that life becomes easy for you. Not to save you, but to save ourselves, we need your help. Lion and I want to surrender before the Police. |
| Satya | : | Has Arun agreed with this decision? |
| Surabhi | : | After thinking a lot, we have decided to give up the S.I.F.O. |
| Satya | : | Thank God. He has shown you the right path. I am ready to help you. Be quick to move out. |
| Surabhi | : | You should be ready to leave this camp anytime at night. We will call you. We will move out together. |
| Satya | : | Alright. I am waiting for you. |

[Surabhi leaves. The Doctor starts sleeping while sitting. The wall clock hints at late night. Bul checks intermittently. Getting an advantage, someone throws a handbag. Doctor Satya picks up that bag and opens it. He sees a torch light, two diaries, some old inland letters, and an envelope bundle from that bag. He also finds a letter written on red paper and reads the letter in torch light. The scenes of throwing bags and reading the letters will be repeated here because Doctor Satya describes his memories of the S.I.F.O. camp before the Journalist Mangaraj. After reading the letter, Arun enters with Alok.]

| | | |
|---|---|---|
| Arun | : | Doctor Sahib, I gave you that handbag and the letter. You move out of the camp first with Alok. Surabhi and I will join you soon. |
| Satya | : | How can I believe that you will join us? |
| Arun | : | Doctor, believe us. Our life has been significant and precious to us. If we leave at once, none of us can live. Please come; I will help you and Alok move out of the camp first. Follow me. |

[Doctor Satya Sanatan and Alok follow Arun. Then the Clock ticks. After sometimes Surabhi and Arun come from opposite directions. They are with rifles.]

| | | |
|---|---|---|
| Surabhi | : | What happened? |
| Arun | : | Doctor Satya Sanatan and Alok wait for us safely outside the camp. We can also escape. |
| Surabhi | : | All the guards outside have already slept. Why will they suspect us? |
| Arun | : | All right. How far have you done the task I have allotted you? |
| Surabhi | : | The entire roof of the camp, the door of the Commander's room, and Bul's room and door are installed with explosives. |
| Arun | : | I have also installed bombs with the Ammunitions Room and brought all the wires to the Battery room. If any problem arises and we switch on the battery, there will be an explosion in the entire camp. You go to that battery room, and I will follow you. |

| | | |
|---|---|---|
| Surabhi | : | Why after me? Let's go together. |
| Arun | : | I have got some sensitive papers from the Commander's room. That proves that the S.I.F.O., receiving money from foreign countries, works here for internal disturbances and chaos and spreading terror and anarchy among our country's people. We will submit all these papers/documents before the Police. You wait, I am coming. |

[Arun leaves. Surabhi waits for Arun. Seeing Bul at a distance, Surabhi hides. After that, Bul and Commander enter.]

| | | |
|---|---|---|
| Commander | : | Have you checked their room? |
| Bul | : | Both Arun and Surabhi are missing, Commander. They are not here. |
| Commander | : | They are somewhere here in the surroundings. We must find them out. |
| Bul | : | I am going on this side. You move on that side. |

[Bul and Commander go in opposite directions. Arun slowly enters with a bag. That bag suddenly slips from his hand, and the papers are dispersed. Keeping the rifle on the ground, Arun collects all the papers and puts them in the bag. At this stage, the Commander enters and orders Arun with his rifle.]

| | | |
|---|---|---|
| Commander | : | Don't move, Lion. Don't try to pick up the rifle. Stand up…come to this side…yes…come to this side. You think you are the only intelligent one here. After releasing Doctor outside, you will leave with Surabhi later. The Chief's instruction |

|  |  |
|---|---|
|  | was to release Doctor. But I tried to take a test of your fidelity to our S.I.F.O. and ordered you to kill Doctor. Both of you were disloyal to me and released Doctor. The Chief's order is executed…but you were red-handed. |
| Arun | : Commander, we won't allow you to kill us painfully…we will never allow you to live here. |
| Commander | : You bastard! I thought of you as a true patriot. But keep in mind nobody returns alive from a terrorist's camp. I will torture you in such a manner that no other Fighters will show any courage to leave the camp. |
|  | [Surabhi suddenly comes with a rifle and stands behind Commander.] |
| Surabhi | : Commander, I will be forced to shoot you unless you drop your rifle. |

[Arun brings Commander to his control before he says anything and snatches the rifle from him.]

| Arun | : Commander, you can no longer lead us with your slogans of patriotism and revolution to a place whose consequences are already black and bleak. You are all receiving massive funds from foreign lands to weaken our country. Foreign countries sponsor terrorism to spread in the land. Now, it is divulged. Stand up there like that. Surabhi, you move fast; I will go. |

[Surabhi, deserting Commander, runs. Bul suddenly fires

her from outside. Surabhi falls and comes out crawling on the stage/ground. Before Arun fires at Bul, he hides himself. The commander suddenly brings his pistol out of his pocket and fires at Arun. Arun falls. The commander happily laughs at the sight of Arun getting shot. At the time of falling, Arun groans in pain.]

Arun : Commander, I know…The entrance gates of this Organization are always open to all, but its exit points are permanently closed. We have already set the bombs and land mines throughout the camp. Nobody can escape. Each room of the camp is installed with explosives. Once we switch on the battery, everything will blast and get ruined.

Commander : Bul…without wasting time, you disconnect all wires. Be quick.

[Commander tries to disconnect the wires with his teeth. Surabhi's voice is heard from a distance.]

Surabhi : Arun, I have already reached the battery room. These people have besieged me here. Before I switch on the battery, you leave the camp if possible. I will bomb down the entire camp before they kill me.

[Commander and Bul start running. But there was an explosion. Commander and Bul are thrown away. In the cyclorama is the scene of a burning fire: Satya Sanatana and Alok act, running before the stage. There is the sound of a train's arrival nearby. Subsequently, the stage light is off. In the darkness, the stanza of Satya Sanatan is heard… Do all sorts of arrangements for Alok today…For he who has lost his path in darkness…]

●●

## For The Director

The director can plan the stage in any style for the play *The Message*. The playwright will have no objection if this play is staged on an open stage. If it is acted on the stage covered by the screens, the following instructions may be kindly paid attention to for more significant influence over the audience.

This play comprises many scenes, such as the residential place of extremists, three different rooms thereof, the Railway station, the Conference Room of Sugreeva Nayak, the Mandap for meeting at *Melana* field, the marine road at the sea beach, the unique places where Surabhi and Arun stay for their letter correspondence, etc. The realistic sets can't be possible on this small stage. The play's staging will be more expensive if the small stage gets extended. Thus, we must create different zones to create a platform for the entire stage. With the control of lights, we must perform the scenes systematically without any break. Considering the location and size of the stage for using different symbols and the illusion of lights on the cyclorama, the director may use two small platforms on the front side of the stage and two big platforms on the back of the stage. He will also allow space between the small and big platforms (i.e., in the middle of the stage). At the back of the stage, just in the middle before the cyclorama on a platform train compartment's symbol, two windows are kept, and before it lies the space where at least two people can sit. Along with the compartment is at a small distance a frame for the T.V. and the seating arrangement of a person behind the frame. The director can show his creativity using different symbolic props for this play.

The play's success depends on continuous rehearsal of the scenes and the natural skill in acting. We will not need costly sets if we can arrange all these props. So, when the actors and actresses get by hearts their respective dialogues, their confidence level will increase to perform, and they will help their audience understand the theme better. Thus, the director and the playwright's effort will be fruitful before the audience.

**Dilliswar Moharana**

**Black Eagle Books**

www.blackeaglebooks.org
info@blackeaglebooks.org

Black Eagle Books, an independent publisher, was founded as a nonprofit organization in April, 2019. It is our mission to connect and engage the Indian diaspora and the world at large with the best of works of world literature published on a collaborative platform, with special emphasis on foregrounding Contemporary Classics and New Writing.

www.ingramcontent.com/pod-product-compliance
Lightning Source LLC
Chambersburg PA
CBHW060618080526
44585CB00013B/892